SELECTED POEMS

from

Unless
God Song: A Grieving Simile
Reluctant Mirrors
Prowling Sequiturs
Proximities
Traces
Taps for Space

DAUBS FOR NEEDY SPACE

Selected Poems

Aaron Rosen

The Sheep Meadow Press
Rhinebeck, NY

Copyright 2017 by Aaron Rosen

All rights reserved. No part of this publication may be reproduced or transmitted in any form or by any means, electronic or mechanical, including photocopy, recording, or any information storage and retrieval system, without permission in writing from the publisher, except in the case of quotations in reviews.

Designed and typeset by The Sheep Meadow Press

Distributed by The University Press of New England

Author Photograph: Carol Harmel
Cover image: after Giulio Romano

Library of Congress Cataloging-in-Publication Data

Names: Rosen, Aaron, 1926- author.
Title: Daubs for needy space : selected poems / Aron Rosen.
Description: Rhinebeck, NY : Sheep Meadow Press, [2017]
Identifiers: LCCN 2017005185 | ISBN 9781937679729 (softcover)
Classification: LCC PS3618.O83 A6 2017 | DDC 811/.6--dc23
LC record available at https://lccn.loc.gov/2017005185

All inquiries and permission requests should be addressed to the publisher:

The Sheep Meadow Press
PO Box 84
Rhinebeck, NY 12572

for my wife,
Toni Peters

Contents

I. UNLESS

Unless	3
After All	5
Belief: A Fable	6
Flesh: An Essay	7

II. GOD SONG: A GRIEVING SIMILE

God Song	11
L'Envoy	25
Every Smile a Simile, Every Simile a Smile: Bow Wow	28

III. *from* RELUCTANT MIRRORS

Leonardo's Wall	33
Reluctant Mirrors	37
Untitled (for Jasper Johns)	44
Before	46
Instead	47
In Other Words	48
Song	49

IV. *from* PROWLING SEQUITURS

A Word in Play	53
So Long / So Far / No See	54
Awash	58
Bad Lighting	60
Just So	67
Prowling Sequiturs	73
Clocks in Their Past Time	78
In Spectral Flight	82
A Very Still Life	84
Small Matter	85
A Poet in Harm's Way	86
Taps for Space 2	87

Lying In	88
Circus Days 2	89
Portrait d'Une Femme	90
An Overnight with Words	91
Still Life with a Half-Truth	92
In Truth	93
Poetry (by All Means)	94
Feelings (Untitled)	97
Cher Nombril	108
French Lessons	109
Pages	110
Poem	113

V. from **PROXIMITIES**

Between the Clock and the Bed	117
Proximities	132
A Conversation	137

VI. from **TRACES**

Traces I	141
Traces II	169
Navelwatch	185
The Tomb of Mallarmé	186
The Pauses	187

VII. from **TAPS FOR SPACE**

Taps for Space	193
"The Man"	196
Images of Vietnam	197
Staying Home	199
On the Frontier	200
Old Hat	202
Reading Ourselves to Sleep	203
Still Life	204
Self-Portraits	205
Hopper	205
Chagall	206
Segal	207

De Chirico	208
Hesse	209
Miró	210
Newman	211
Rothko	212
Avery	213
Twombly	214
Matisse	215
Gottlieb	216
Arp	217
Magritte	218
Cézanne	219
Rauschenberg	221
Kline	222
Balthus	223
Schiele	224
Giacometti	225
Malevitch	226
Braque	227
Oldenburg	228
An *Après le Bain* Lithograph	229
Fresh Widow	230
Ótages	231
Cézanne's Apples	232
Odalisque	233
The Concert	234
Le Déjeuner sur L'Herbe	235
The Chinese Trade	236
Allotments	237
A Version of Pastoral	238
A Race of Metaphor	239
Circus Days	240

I.
UNLESS

UNLESS

Unless belief escape within quotes all signs of lying
Unless the self contained without question come undone
Unless life in pantomime explore the silence it belongs to
Unless illusion wear its eyes out
Unless the theatre of accuracy pursue the silence in question
Unless words like exposed hideouts be laid to rest
Unless out in the cold a branch un-birding sing
Unless a password languishing in bye-bye lend an ear
Unless language explain its mirror's blindside
Unless coincidence look life in the eye
Unless credulity passed over in silence become a reason in disguise
Unless words in their wisdom go without saying
Unless a fine collage make for a body's grounding
Unless illusions forget where they've come from
Unless a self absorbed in error fine-tune a thought without mercy
Unless memory wear a child on its sleeve
Unless happiness left to die keep the lights on all night
Unless patience seem a shadow short of sleep
Unless life like a stray ending follow a map of contrition
Unless images have eyes to hide
Unless truth like a parable go incognito
Unless in writing it exploit a ubiquitous detour
Unless a body emptied of summer stand poised to remember
Unless ennui escape its sorry mirror
Unless a sigh for sore eyes embrace a witness
Unless a vertiginous likeness overstay all foreplay
Unless in memory it overtake reflection
Unless careers riddle the airs they author
Unless a book-length abbreviation add to our dismay
Unless gender quickly aging deny the sentence

Unless words fasting to distraction spurn all signs of life
Unless hard-pressed in a book they spell a life in retreat
Unless a plague of meaning escape to the place where everything is true
Unless.

AFTER ALL

Are wants words lost sight of after
all rumors of discounted flesh
are only memories of the rest
of life where all haunts are done for.

Impatient with immortality,
we keep time for each change of heart,
and grief-stricken under a cloud
pursue words for some ungodly resolution.

But a cloud looks in its anecdotage
to no wonder after all mishaps
in haunting our unsightly wants
are lost without a word to a blind reflection.

After all appearances are found
wanting our denatured flesh
to hold harmless all our haunts
to pursue in words the wants we overtake in wonder.

BELIEF: A FABLE

    I.
To forget now to believe
as before how no telling
meets the eye, how aged
in wonder a prolonged
look evokes no evidence
but a ghostly qualm appears
within reason a prompting
shadow to impersonate
the imaginary, in effect,
the disappearance that detains us without cause.

    II.
Just so belief finds its
force in knowing how
a metaphor evokes in error
the imaginary, in effect,
bedding a cloud in hard time.
Here shivering in our "good night,"
we fall to our knees
an impromptu ruin
as desire counts chapter verse
the disappearance that detains us without cause.

    III.
Belief lies only in theory where
the time saved for crying out
loud is absent
absentmindedness
more lonely than before
we explored charity with –
Heavens above – the tall tale
that riddles the heart
in practice only the disappearance that detains us without cause.

FLESH: AN ESSAY

So out of order the flesh was was
true to the word it keeps forgetting
how the lonely acrobat of its dreams
finds in his frequent ceiling some repose.
So flesh where it counts words
compares reason at a loss
to the fascination that was
out of order quick to confess
a sameness soon forgotten.

So each pound mirrored in another's
cause is caught in the image that was like
the like-minded reason left behind was
true to the emptiness it keeps forgetting.

So it was, taking nothing
to heart, an emptiness
true to the word it leaves behind.
Self-taught, it declares flesh
weighed down by its shadow
out of order, an heirloom past forgetting.

So words here remember to forget
that flesh without reason contains
the one image that was was
emptied of the stillness now forgotten.

So truth to be sure leaves
on holiday, its cause aghast.
Spirited away in a word made
ready, it measures the discontinuous
flesh missed but not forgotten.

So each pound of reason, revealed
in the image of an acrobat, is caught
eavesdropping on the emptiness
of a mindless verb long since forgotten.

So flesh that wordless widow of excess
is found in devotion to return all favors
to an emptiness that out of order
seems a comfort past forgetting.

So it is a world emptied of all
gratuitous wit that out of order
the word finds urgent. Its cause,
the flesh, its misgivings
reach out to the lonely acrobat
pinned to the frequent ceiling of his dreams.

So out of order a passer-by
might find in the sight-lines of this mind
his flesh turning every which way
to measure the emptiness he leaves behind
in the alliteration that was was
the only voice the heart made fonder
out of the order he keeps forgetting.

II

GOD SONG
A GRIEVING SIMILE

GOD SONG 1

In truth his words like peevish gods
devour speech, repeat
in dumbshow their innocence.
Furtively, they mate in a sweet hereafter.

On the brink of ubiquity
they find in nature
a hungry ghost
the face of heartbreak
that feeds on error
and awkwardly rouses art from stupor.

In their blind sightings
words
lonely in the memory
become in truth candor's fig leaf.
So, in error, innocence
pardons reason without mercy
till art in desperation comes of age.

GOD SONG 2

Is god then among consenting words
a pause, a mis-
begotten loneliness
who in appearance
would tempt space
fret without reason
longing to get away

from the bruised word
that out of some impassioned humdrum
invents a future.
In its apprehension –
no quarter given –
it takes our breath away.

In the cathedral of the absolute
each departing pause
is in truth
not one for words
an appearance found wanting.

GOD SONG 3

Words swear by inclement gods.
In their apprehension
they alight the scene
eyeing nature in its stunned debut.

In the economy of the unrequited
like-minded words
fidget in their high redoubt
and borrow from nature

by grace of silence
a witness to the unremembered life
shredding speech
with its artful verbs of prey.

GOD SONG 4

On God-watch, his words
deprived of destiny
rejoice in the mischief of the unsaid.

With unrelenting hindsight, he
under the spell of a sly clock,
filibusters time's death-wish
his words now manhandled to no end.

Greedy for face-time,
his words, afraid to be lost,
rally to a faith-in-waiting.
Lingering in ungodly space
they become in time
the humbug of departure
a difficult collage.

GOD SONG 5

Orphaned now
in their silver lining
his words become like ornaments
fond siblings
of inarticulate regret.

Does truth then
fail appearance
conceal in words
a spent godling
or within reason
a poet's plunder in intimate display.

GOD SONG 6

Alone in gravity's diaspora
his words in unrequited space
disquiet speech,
discard the distance
a fraught godling
might keep for himself so long.

Heard in the growling of the universe
words
like desperate oaths
disappoint reality in vain.

GOD SONG 7

Are words then
like tangled oaths
hostage to the end of life.
Stranded in their knowingness
they engage space
spell the distance
an endless child discards at last in vain.

For company, they'd plumb
the rumor of God's Word –
in its intimacy
an artless pretext –
to mimic speech instead.

GOD SONG 8

God in a word
risks all
becomes in truth a vacancy
trope-free to wit.

Our words now
spirited away in a blind bemuse
become in truth our self-regard
where two-time godlings
prey on future's past.
Bereft of wit we are word-proof at last.

GOD SONG 9

Featherbedding the absolute
words inherit the future to a fault.
Like reviled godlings
they enter the picture
vandalize
the Father of Faces,
to become in faith
the impossible occult of his halo
the estranged irony of history
the uninhabitable memory of a word.

GOD SONG 10

Spellbound in the light of fiction
a distraught pronoun
besot with relevance
is, out of earshot,
the ghost of a living memory.
It gropes its way to rhyme
with the first person, the one
who, on a blind watch,
finds in his self-regarding irony, an innocence
an eyelash short
that expatriates the truth.

GOD SONG 11

Scruples that trick out
his otherness
host in a grace note
a word-beleaguered wit:
a blithe godling
whose lyric innocence
dedicates
to the marriage of why
the ghost of history
his vigilant absence
his art.

GOD SONG 12

Words in their non-committal negligee
embrace every gaudy pause.
In their mother tongue
they frisk each hapless truth
yours truly
for an echo of recognition.
Heartbreaking in the absolute
delirious in their innocence
they grace the melodic calendar of pain.

GOD SONG 13

Was god once
a hopeful monster.
In his knowingness
did he eat the darkness whole

to become at last
a deathless dazzle
a desperate truth
surrounded by a shudder.

Then as if
what goeth before
blindsided by a predatory faith
all godlings who out of luck
come after exhale their pride in art.

GOD SONG 14

In the cemetery of their endless knowing
the gods are grieving similes.
Bespoke they pander to the accidental
riddle the air with benedictions
in malady memorize all said and done for
a left over word to wit:
a shady lady
changing the unstroked hours.

L'ENVOY

    1.
Hear now
how God is
a sketch, a wistful actor
a *bon farceur* who deploys words, celebrities all, as decoys.

Hear how
incumbent mindfuls rest assured,
how in evidence
godlings, bedfellows all, muse in the shadows.

    2.
Let *Like* ponder likeness,
face-to-face pander laughter
in all likelihood create
a kinship in belief.
Let godlings at their own peril
take shelter absentmindedly
in a grace of mind and bring it all
back – their sorry heads held high –
meticulously home.

    3.
Something untoward: a thought
a precocious likeness wanting
to be seen among godlings
as a word of artful expertise.
Like unsparing in its godliness
each likeness a daub of needy space
excerpts thoughtfulness.
Everything that passes for time
celebrates incontinence,
the soulful face of unforgetting, happily remiss.
Life's daring-do artfully undone.

4.
Laughter
bedrock of unlikelihood
disputes
a lapsed shadow waiting
for a god
to imperceptibly make up his mind
here where gravity's laughter
becomes improbably
an estranged likelihood-in-waiting.
Daubs of mercy
miraculously mistaken
are found recuperating in jeopardy's aesthetics:
gravity's laughter
a god's fond farewell.

5.
Hanging about the corner of his eye
a smile, a face –
a face to live up to –
a reason to believe
how Art in its heaven –
with its secret belief in its own unconcern
might imperfectly decorate
every godling's face
with gravity's laughter
a god's fare-thee-well.

6.
Belief
having found no word for laughter
takes direction from a soul's grimace
and finds in a sketch a blowhard echo,
a do-over likeness.

In the deep of a spirited mirror
a word
a pledge
disfigures those stray days
caught in the eye swimming with indifference –
each word adhering to the nearest shadow.

Here god speaks well of indifference
and with nothing in mind
reaffirms the likeness in every dolor –
feigning regret –
a belief's addiction.

EVERY SMILE A SIMILE, EVERY SIMILE A SMILE: BOW WOW

    1.

Lies and the like gnaw thoughtfully on the bone.
Belief alights at the nearest shadow.
Absentmindedly it startles a mirror full of looks,
drowns there in static.
Alone in the room, a posse of shadows
its viewpoint unanimous.
Dog tired with regret
innocence extracts a legacy from presumption's bite:
a word to the wise
is a word of prey.
Woof, woof!

    2.

Do questing mirrors borrowed from
belief's lookalike (in all likelihood
a godling's understudy) hunt in needy similes
for tales of shaggy disbelief.
Here dogs in their bleak surmise wise up
to some exacting vacancy –
where fraught godlings rally in their cups
to a dog's life
spent barking up the wrong tree.
Go fetch!

    3.

Lies at length dog the length of the day.
They candidly bark
till blue in the face.
All smiles are lost in candor's doghouse

where deadpan similes bespeak shadows,
thoughtfully guard all life's intersections,
watch for shortcuts,
and spuriously hunt God's cunt in a funk –
each ghostly simile a sigh of remorse.
Here echoes matter till spirited away,
come to grief in blue's respite.

    4.
Is life then a grieving historian
whose ghostly needs
smilingly mock a likeness on its hind legs.
Here, in a funk, every meanwhile expires –
godspeed
where every vowel is a vow
helplessly out of space
and where echoes like gods
in the not too distant future
are mockingly,
surreptitiously left for dead,
whistling their belief in life's doggone sequiturs.
BOW WOW!

    5.
Meticulously intervening here
among grieving sequiturs
space becomes the next to last word,
a spare chance
only the shadow knows.
Dogging *whatever*
samples space
vamps a likeness
a dogmatic singular.
BOW WOW!

      6.
Tellingly what words accomplish belief regrets.
(Every simile a smile every smile a simile.)
Unerringly forlorn words frown.
Interlopers all,
they head for the nearest shadow
to sulk there
in their ghostly aura of disbelief.

The last word left for dead.
BOW WOW!

III
from *RELUCTANT MIRRORS*

LEONARDO'S WALL

If you pause in the realization of pictorial forms and look at the spots on the wall, at the ashes of the hearth, at the clouds . . . on careful observation you will make wonderful discoveries there.
—Leonardo da Vinci

    I.
You stare down
In the face of being
The unbecoming
Spot that compares all signs of life
With eternity.
Patience, standing on its own
Shadow, startles the wall.
It sweats horizons
Open to the touch of your hand.

    II.
Does a sign, true to the wall,
Look after the unforeseen
Chance of a wreck, the un-
Becoming HERE unmasked
As an unassuming glyph –
The trace of a hand,
Or a wound that measuring the horizon's
Outlook, enters the picture
Without conscience.

    III.
A gesture preserved
Where all inference ends
Announces your originality.
An urgent shadow
Pregnant with foreplay,

It riddles the wall,
And spotting each hush,
Becomes a mirror to your belief.

    IV.

Hope is the One
Duration lip-synchs.
White as a wish, it extracts
A cloud that returns
All gestures to a palimpsest
Where hexes of ash
Like some intimate syntax
Pulse with a loss at hand.

    V.

Drawn from the ashes of solicitude,
Home's body's afire.
It recalls a face
An abandoned hope –
All patience aglow
Face to face
With an angel brought to mind.

    VI.

A hand that kindles a mind-
Harboring intimacy without like
Recovers space as a burnt
Offering, or a spent
Collage that altering thought
Authors an ash of its own.

    VII.

Ash is the discipline of all
Cognition, where each burning
Idea, faced with a reflux

Of angels, awaits reflection.
Words, hiding their exhilaration,
In faltering light
Measure the wall's shortfall.

VIII.
An abyss of gestures hoarding
Angels pleads for the end
Of time, where all symbols,
Mingling with rainbows, bed
In the next world your solemn
Look to resume the life
The wall upholds by an eyelash.

IX.
Eyes that forget
The anniversary of a wound
Are blind to the touch.
Surrounded by neglect,
They find an originality
In the royal rawness of a wronged angel,
A grand nostalgia befriended by a name for nearness.

X.
It's the old argument for precedence . . .
Peeled from an imitation
Of solitude, eyes,
Given a thought,
Shadow all their inadequacy.
Their lust overcast,
They make up –
Legible only to closed eyes –
A face in abeyance: a wall.

XI.
Your unsigned reason sleeps
Like a sullen cloud,
A shrouded spot.
Faced with a world that wanes,
Nausea's a thought
A stale pulse
Shadowing a bleak façade.

XII.
Are unblinking spots there-
Fore the clouds of our intelligence?
A cloud as if
To face up to
The vestige of an aspiration
Turns to the wall
And seems to witness our belief . . .
A blinding shadow,
It sweats an eternity at large.

RELUCTANT MIRRORS

After Susan Rothenberg

From repetition was born not uniformity but sense, accident.
– Jean Frémon

    1.
A part wrapped in its outcome
Is a face strewn across speech.

Told that way, read
As a wrong-way face,
It calls to a reckless window
Exhaling space,
A wry accident come out of hiding.

    2.
Stripped from sight,
Can a window facing scrutiny
Deny departure, descry
By accident the brave part of hiding
The distance found in evidence
Beset by red
But visibly overlooked.

    3.
Is an accident but a solemn gesture
In forgetful light
The unseen part of speech?
Its blind side
The far eye of a horse
Dismantles distance
The window's faltering rhyme.

4.
Windows fall short
Bereft of all horizons.
Fragments lie about
Outgrow the horizon
Studious to a fault.
Each mishap bends moonlight
To look for a caress.

5.
Chance laid out
As an accident explains
Sleep as a wronged eyeful,
In unkempt light,
The perspiring ghost of
A lost moment
Inherits an end in sight.

6.
But flattering chance
(To put a face on it)
An accident,
Its bemused image,
Nothing but a feeling's overhang,
In turning back
Surprises the view.

7.
A window by an open mind
Declines a deep analysis of red,
Its wronged look
Deployed as an empty thought.
Now using everything in sight,
Speech as a life-sized mirror
Comes out of hiding.

8.
Will chance left to itself
Find a destination just breathing.
Its shadow healing in the doorway,
An outcome stranded
In borrowed light,
It turns away
That a once-over world come begging.

9.
A figure alive to a wild guess
Looks upon windows with impatience
Enlarging candor.
It's the idle part of waiting
Defies utterance,
The envy of memory,
Where no image applies.

10.
Windows have no idea.
They speed thought past
Like accidents in a mirror.
Here words sweat peace.
They rally to the horizontal,
Their red residue
The defaced part: the longing.

11.
An immaculate suicide
Eyes a manic blue yonder.
The broken part of being
Left behind repairs
Space outlives chance
In its innocence
The outside of a sigh.

12.
Darling of distance,
The horizon waits like a borrowed memory
A look-a-like reduced to unused sleep.
Death being a rumor
Apart from the dust that settles
On its nakedness
Finds its language in a blind trust.

13.
In the death of a true description,
The aggrieved voice
Having lost its place
Finds a first person
Buried in thought.
With a fine simplicity,
It makes a mirror its escort.

14.
Will the vocative of the unforeseen
Explain coincidence,
Assign to the light
The precise sex of darkness?
In expiring space
Forgetfulness
Is the autobiography of chance.

15.
The corpse, a first-hand shadow,
Mirrors all gender-debris.
Assigned a room,
It departs in a bleak aside,
A forgetful echo.
The horizon, rhymed into blindness,
Resigns all windows to tears.

16.
A pause, a petulant half-
Forgotten abstract blue
Truce, given a chance,
Lingers too long in the truth.
It gives voice
To an accident
That shadows silence like a criminal.

17.
Each false start
Predicts the future.
A letter arrived at
By accident
Will stare down
In memory
The calligraphy of a slant torso.

18.
The narrative of a chance-
In-waiting lies in the archives of a yawn.
Is an accident
But a wronged vowel?
Stored in the blood,
It extracts from the onset of duration
An abrupt shadow parting.

19.
In the name of forgetfulness,
The accident ends in a bleak mirror,
The blood absent on the face of it,
A long night out of tears.
Dreaming itself to sleep,
Reason in bed with a fiery sunset
Has the dry-eyed look of death.

20.
An accident with an eye
To console ravishes
Chance. Given a hand,
In the light of no exception,
It grooms hearsay –
All four legs rhyming –
With a sidelong reticence out of sight.

21.
A window's oversight in depth
Finds an accident run aground.
In preserved light,
Faced with a downcast parting of limbs,
The trope, a stranded mirror,
Studies the unforeseen
Meaning to stand alone.

22.
The forgetful part is being
Itself a shy conceit. The abrupt
Hoof dreaming of indecision
Is emptied of an unexpected depth.
Here chance befalls
A lost footfall
Like a crying rhyme.

23.
The pause that exhorts the unfinished
Dark is the vocative that wants
To hide. It defers only –
No accident – to a wide-spread
Silence, the hoofs
Sounding in the tedium
Left behind.

24.
Chance harboring all
Extinction sits by the window
Like a sly mirror.
Foresight's a saddle much traveled
Where maturity
At eye's reach
Has the cogent look of an accident.

25.
Will an outcome held in readiness
Free an accident with a past?
Rumored until read,
It evokes its part
As a staged coda.
Embraced by chance,
It lasts how long it comes to rest in a word.

UNTITLED (FOR JASPER JOHNS)

    I.
Here brushstrokes weathering space
brood over your idle airs.
Like dubious clouds,
well-versed in your unconcern,
they refuse the life that dawns on us
losing out to the lay of the land.
But open to low-lying conundrums,
your devoted particulars lie in wait
like solemn oaths
whispering what remains of space
your body grooms in a crime scene
as a ghostly speculation.

    II.
In widowed carcasses
you hide a jealous silhouette
and, given cause, find
in error all weather lost
in the oeuvre of your self-
regard where suffering
a dubious good
night you mind the place,
smothered by tears,
a posthumous collage
affirms: your self al fresco.

    III.
Ahead of all longing,
you return reason
to the desecration
of a breathless future

where shrouded in sighs,
you eye in exile ahead
of all things, a doubt
aging among explanations.
With a long face,
you extol in earnest
the effort of carcasses
with their vague memory of fatigue.

BEFORE

All terminations are photo-ops for good.

Flushed with visitations,
they look to the eye
and just so
arrest plenty
to arrive at nothing more
than a dream of prey where love's
a forethought after
all a reminiscence
the spent present
of a shapeless time before.

Scheduling hindsight
as a prop between
flaws that lengthen
the body so
monotony
catching the eye of love
just so a photo-op
might after all
suffer its image
as a terminus

until it leaves in another's look for good.

INSTEAD

About the body
all memory is –
time at a loss –
a misplaced future.
We enter speech
filibustering a lost cause.

Here the body lingers –
time at a loss –
fathering instead
the ruins of artifice
where memories
like a lost cause
are curiosities of the soul.

So a body is –
time at a loss –
like memory
a late riser.
We become instead
the spare exit
to a lost cause

so continue like love to cease.

IN OTHER WORDS

It's the keening of no known text
decorates insomnia.
Put at a loss,
our shadow-play like a blind saying
widows the visible
in other words
the shape of the poem
but a murmur stored in a flagrant body.

Disguised as a whim,
we monitor
each complication of readiness
as a snug fit
hard to pronounce
in other words
a sharp reproach to visibility
leaking wide-eyed into the future.

SONG

Let flowers name
After long being
One for the road

An absence urging
Loudly in bed
A would-be figure of speech.

Each name's a promise
Found gathering
Unwilling flowers, hearts,

Names to undo habits
Perhaps to copy
The final blush

We forget ourselves
In order to pledge a head.

IV

from *PROWLING SEQUITURS*

A WORD IN PLAY

Just now a word
while eavesdropping on the absolute
is enthralled to a wise unsaid.

In gala pretense
it finds in hearsay
no memory of its own
but the ghost of relevance
where the dream of language
is an airy-eyed lullaby
an angel's invisible hug.

Here in a paradise of loose ends
its solemn bygones
abandoned to translation
cry foul.

SO LONG / SO FAR / NO SEE

. . . within shadows—
so long no see—the un-
doing, at first blush,
of a bed made up
to audition blindness
a sight past due: a photograph!
where body language
eyes indiscretion as
an epitaph and scraps
of memory in exactitude
stop breathing non-
sequiturs of a sight on stage
so long.

Are images so far
an effort of memory
gone wrong?
Alarmingly innocent
they overstay the loss that blinds us
to abide in a borrowed look.
Figuring absence so
long equanimity is last
seen as the object past caring.

Joined in pronunciation
the image in progress
drawn to insomnia
idles at wits end.
Gala in exile
it woos syntax so
long that a pulse plucked
from incurable space
where lapsed speech

flourishing in non-sequiturs
extracts happiness so far
a bluebird with the spent look of belonging.

In blue skies
bluebirds keep to themselves
their longing, refresh
their distance in lost time.
Absent images, they
assign shadows ahead
of all things caught dreaming
alongside – good grief –
a happiness so far unseen.

Here sight's familiar shades
truth, under the weather
replenishes the blue.
So time so far behaves
in nature like a photograph
that choosing distance imagines
loss. A career sighs,
pleading a life in error.

So far the word, a blue sighting,
looks like a blank stare.
Image-ready, it loses sleep
raising objections with no
time on which to rest
unseen: so long a thought,
just a thought orphaned
like a photograph an afterlife clouds over.

Now images feud. Their anonymity,
attached to shadows, recalls
how, so long rephrased in

pantomime, they shed a thought
so far-sighted that lost
in wonder they find time
to multiply a complicit
blue so long it makes you cry.

Seeing happiness so far
borrows from time
an inference of choice.
A photograph covets it
silvering its air
of equanimity
till a blind so long surrenders
all to a fond memory of self.

A breath so far a thought-
sighting repeats so long
a life in syllables.
They die in camera –
an oath upon them –
orphaning
in quick time
images of a blue regret.

Do thoughts so far akin
collect their images in quotes
or, as in a photograph,
bed with all
absences in question
to multiply
foreshadowings so long
an orphanage of choice.

A photo so taken
in full cry
interprets lust

as, take for take,
an image that so far
blindsighted
in adultery
beds in memory
a gesture so long
a euphemism for choice.

Seconded by sight so long
past due, a photograph
admits a choice shadowed
by indiscretion.
Each shame-faced gesture
is just a thought, in memory
an epitaph, romancing
a life so far so long.

So hindsight reasons for company
with a life so long
a posthumous site
that a sigh stranded
in its blue pretext
becomes a lookout for sore eyes.
They flash our feelings as they stalk
time with its unused loss to bed.

Seeing as how its blind eye
turns to its once upon
unsightly happiness,
the photograph so long
a refuge for a lost thought
samples in its vernacular
a look-see, the guilty
ghost of the only life there is.

AWASH

Somebody missed
nobody for good
but a thing said
is everywhere to quote
an image named after
a blind trust.
Awash with coincidence
the limit of the world
is an effort to stay in sight.

So inventive is absence
that accuracy
awash in flight
from nobody's calling
is the eye's misuse
for company
of the last word
spent knowing
what somebody said for good.

Nothing said
to speak to
nobody's need
to extract from vanity
the missing chance
that an image might
limiting insight
be somebody's fate
awash all along for good.

Images that miss
in great detail
what's said in solace

awash within hearing
of another life
at last recall
what nobody minds:
the unmirrored fate
of somebody's wish in vain.

Nobody's shy
exit in sight
is a thing said
to repeat itself
summoning chance
awash in a last laugh.
So rhymes that die
in dialogue
find somebody missed in vain for good.

It gets late early here
when cheek to cheek
what sigh convicts
freedom awash
in its own sweet time
grants to somebody's
spellbound touch
the perfect fit
what's said instead in nobody's sight.

BAD LIGHTING

Beds that visit
in bad lighting
handicap a living
image out of sorts.

In latency
lyric pastimes
tattoo their never minds
to dark applause.

And loneliness
like a blind eye
that never minds
the lighting turns
instead in errancy
to the orphaned eye
of a fine grief
come home at last to seed.

Taken to bed in throes
icons of never mind
put a shadow under
their intimacy
that out of its skin
provides a pastime
a loneliness
where limb to limb
addicts of bad lighting
execute
for the last time
a fanfare of bone.
(Here imagery
describes nothing
but a blindness brought to bed.)

Intimacy
the widowed origin
of every snatch
accompanies
bad lighting.
It beds with small talk
makes of pastime
a pavane of dark consent.
In loneliness
existence stares
interpretation down
bares in its thoughts
a prayer
for an unused bed out of reach.

And so a bed
made up to understand
how an oath in mind
with no face after
goes lame.

Mirrors away
a rash of images
born of inattention
puts a never mind
with the bed's share
that executes
in the creak of its location
a body count
where the guests of loneliness
queue in bad lighting
and heartbreak carries the tune.

Unsung
passion's pronoun
with no verb in sight
is bedridden
with ellipsis.
So cupidity
the guest of every wish
is unstrung
its aftermath
the ambient absence
that collects itself
at the bed's rite
and yields its history
with no thought to spare
the nakedness
that befalls pastime aghast.

Voyeur of origins
these martyred bedtimes
scapegoat bad lighting
while far from the story
anxious shifters
vocalize
a widowhood of signs
grooming impromptu
others to distraction.
Each life a ruse
in its imagery
weathers pastime
as a blind eye
in its intimacy
captures the mind.

Beds that fall
in matching metaphors
for absence
dream on their own
of small wonders.
Guessing at bedclothes
they seem like ghosts
the debris of pastime
in bad lighting
where nakedness
as self-knowledge
changes its name
and intimacy
finds a metonym
marooned in their recognitions.

In consultation, beds
cradle our sayings
in the accident of choice.
Vamping sleep
they call out
a face on duty
that comes to mind
as a badly lit
welcome — a *code blue*
that lends a myth
to nakedness.
Accepting pastime
as *mis-en-scene*
a latency
invites an absence on all fours.

A bed at risk
conceals in its telling
the fate of metaphor
the bedrock promise

to never mind
the slow onset of lust.
In bad lighting
intimacy
a bespoke image
weathers the migration of longing
where beleaguered pastime
suffers a self-
inflicted lyric
a blind prayer
that now shares its calling.

Beds that weigh
happenstance
so lightly
live out their tics
as a sigh might
migrate from hope
to hope to silence
an appetite at risk
that intimacy
might visit grief
and in its errancy
as an orphaned wound
survive the bad lighting.

Stymied by eclogues of astute bedsprings
beds in the bargain
are revisionary
their knowingness
an artifact of lighting.
In this intimacy
frantic nothings
speak from memory
of a bed's caress.

Here in the rut of deprived speech
loneliness
reflects all
being in sight
and half-hearted metaphors
in their errancy
are left looking.

Passing fancies
a frequency to bed
the drowning look
that brings to light
sub rosa
the never mind
that forfeits bedtime out of hand.
At the deep end
a lonely verb
migrates instead
an intimacy
the wreck of an appetite at hand.

(Can a stranded swallow
losing sight of summer
without a clue
resuscitate in sunlight
what amnesty is not.)

Drawn to memory
the bed's share
is beside itself
in the bad lighting
a pastime
where a homemade promise—
duration's trope—

explores in vain
an intimacy
slept through.
(Exactly so
in memory
a denatured swallow
summering in vain.)

Here words—
acoustic bandages—
confront a bedtime's
intimacy apart

from iterations
of lonely clues
shadowy decoys
that sport at bedtime
an imagination apart

that a scheme of language
might orchestrate
in bad lighting
a scherzo of shadows at rest.

JUST SO

To age slowly as you approach the child.
          —Jean Frémon

Fathers sons
whatever comes to mind
their immaturity
makes out from hunger
just so
a rage foregone
in imitation.
Here naming names
its own poison
exacts a stutter
from appearances—
a finesse of fathers
sons not yet
an aftermath at last.

A slight of fathers
sons sized up
just so they wear
the stain of silence
on their sleeves
and make a famine
out of leapt-up hearts
where for the asking
flesh speaks words
just so.
On their blind watch
they decorate
promiscuously
a state of mind.

Out of wordplay
fathers sons
made up like clues
just so
they scout a mirror's
blindside in the know
and take heart
where history
abides flesh
as an unfamiliar
shadowing
just so in imitation
it starves on its own.

The trace of
forever's un-
becoming fathers
sons who commit
truth to untried
syllables
that comes calling
on its own reconnaissance –
each guest
a ghost now
and just so
is godsend to a simile
a mirror lost in flesh.

Fathers sons
in the wreck of language
appear themselves
as metaphors—
each mistake
an identity—

and just so
conclude a home past due.
Taking comfort
from authority
a child's play
bespeaks a mirror
for crying out loud
doubling their loss with speech.

Chance may linger
at a loss confide
in language just
so fathers sons
might rhyme as well
their origins
with a missing look
just so to brook
in scoring speech
a shadow play
that takes instruction
precociously
from stuttering
instead.

Do fathers sons
keep for sake
their yesterdays
and just so
break for bread
their liberty
that makes of imitation
but an accident of choice.
Here distance is
a knockabout

a show dance
that keening mimes
just so
it brings a mirror's trespass to bed.

Discreetly starved
of circumstance
a look just so
escapes itself in the mirror.
Has truthfulness
a mind of its own
in its innocence
upon a time
once betrayed
is generously unforgiving.
Food for a son's
left-over thoughts
fathers a deadpan
understudy.

Father's the un-
finished thought
the unconditional
of whatever meets the eye.
Idol of loneliness
he objectifies
chance in a word
that retrieves a son's
dark enterprise.
Just so
surprised by doubt
he interrupts
half-heartedly
milk spilled along the way.

Absence that makes
of the heart its own
earnest fathers
the son's onset
with arias of doubt.
Just so
it finds in language
an intimacy
that all the same
looks the part on cue.
Is fate the apprentice
of how things are
shadows of what already
is between fathers sons an art.

The arts of honesty
fast just so
fathers sons
in their own language
offer a likeness
to taste
before the taking
the same chance meaning
the son in question
who all the same
answering to
his innocence
might just so
go the extra mile instead.

Fathers sons
in their intimacy
feast on mismatched candor.
In fossil time

they find just so
an honesty in waiting.
Now shadowing
inaccuracy
their emptiness
magics meaning
that beside itself
with imagery
famishes
instead.

Out of sorts
ghosts of the un-
pronounceable
who fathers
sons in all candor
perspires in its dark address.
Here, God knows,
arts of all sorts
are failed galas
in their origins
elegies
of their own making
sons dying out
just so.

PROWLING SEQUITURS

   (After Magritte)

In your museum of unused silence
a child's lookout embraces
laughter with the unnecessary
look it brought to the other
foot that dropped with an un-
told loss in mind.
Among these ruined rhymes
horizons memorize
your solemn shadow
in the silence lost
to a blind bit of thought.

At ease your windows
drop within reason
their intentions
out of sight
that even bygones
mistaking silence for unused
laughter chose a life
without words.
(Here the horizon
a die-hard future
has lost its argument with ease.)

At stake, a child-
like indiscretion
flirts with the unused
grief reasoning
behind your back.
Changing spaces,
the horizon's blind

incontinence—
a dumb-show—
puts a life-like thought
your silence out of reach.

Silence in being
your vernacular
finds in a child
all thought at a loss
a utopia of unreason.
Here rhymes made up
to commit laughter
contain apples, bowlers
in their ghost-like holes where clouds
face off in their own light
horizons of lost sleep.

Clouds
their minds made up
abide a rhyme's farewell
where unused thoughts,
migrating clues,
trace laughter back to a blue
façade. Here a wild guess
inherits reason
your treachery recalls at length
as the imagery
of a pipe out of hand.

Abundant farewells
rhyme with the id's
verdict. Without
question the light
imagines a lost shadow.
Picturing the body's

immaculate limit
it beggars up close
a last laugh.
The horizon,
a dark read, completes
the vacancy in your piece of mind.

The intimacy
of the eye's hideout
descries logic
as the booby scrap
of your lost laughter.
Here shy thoughts
like unused footsteps
circle the halo
of the wounded self.
The horizon measures
what the eye knows by heart.

Is your child the horizon
of unused faith
the lucidity
that collapses history to laughter.
As afterthought
it leaves its mark
a malingering image
of your lost ties—
vicissitudes
of the half life
time leaves behind for laughter.

Far from being
a thought, molested
platitudes
your nudes

lie with honesty
as bald faced buts.
As diatribes
they assign to laughter
the error that invents
you whose silence tellingly
feeds on a bone dry wit.

So fetishes
the décor of thresholds
sigh with the unsaid.
For the sake of laughter
they worry, apart
from meaning, those images
that invite words
in despair of an unused silence.
Recalling error
with the best will
you welcome them on cue.

Laughter having to live
with itself arrives
at length with its antecedents
at the threshold of a poem.
Like stranded weather
it abides the weight
of the anecdotal:
those unwitting thoughts
surplus ghosts
that cross the horizon
with its cast of revelations.

Exiting laughter
an estranged silence
sweats boundaries
for that reason
becomes your say-so
in images.
They commit logic
to your good nights
where usable errors
make sly proposals
a casualty of calm.

CLOCKS IN THEIR PAST TIME

In obscurity
itinerant chance
hoards at clockface
what clarity loathes
holding at length
as a thought apart
a sin to caress.
So a late pastime
sweats dogma
cancels its ghosts
bent on description.
It's the chronic life
abstracts hardship
the horizon maps to a fault.

It happens among clocks
the need to weep
to convert clarity
to a thought at fault
to believe in seeing
at full length
that no dogma
is not to caress
but to outlaw chance
to hoard in bull's eye
a chronic pastime
that a touch of hardship
might eye to eye
greet in the abstract disbelief.

Familiarity
like a chronic ghost
evokes hazard
with poetry.
It hoards within reason
what clocks caress
as souvenirs
of an absolute
conviction.
Seeing believing
what arrests sex
with an eyeful
mistakes reflection
for love's myopic pastime.

Absence collects
ghosts as needed
one caress at a time
and stages so
their vanity
that a lapsed clock
copying sex
might face to face
in the abstract come due.
(Departures' objects
hoard belief
for company
they watch their weight
utterly in paint.)

Let's say said clock
strands sex
and in the abstract
's gone to sleep
with objectivity.
In memory
as the eyes have it
a blind guess
might come to share
desire's bathos
or its confidant
a pastime
and depart let's say,
with apprehension.

Unclocked just so
a chronic life
afflicts no matter what
absent matter
compares itself
in the dead of light
to an unintended tale
that sunning itself
in its own night
falls to be sure
all over itself
to caress just so
in metonym
all matter so in sight.

Hoarding obscurity
a clock in its pastime
has come to matter
as an untold silence
at liberty.
Here a pause in defense
of clarity—
a hazard wrapped
in its own words—
endures speech
as the dogma of intention.
And wry dreams
like chronic nocturnes
form letters of credit.

Untended readings, wounds
of unkempt surfaces
hosting signs
of old dogmas
reform angles of concupiscence
sly proximities
defeated in translation.
Like stranded clocks
they consume clarity
where chance hoarding
a last wish
is a chronic absence
a nocturnal nothing
that reconstitutes a pastime.

IN SPECTRAL FLIGHT

Doves that fail your heart's
desire at full cry
interrupt
my fetish of nothing seen.
In spectral flight
their velocity
is lost in no time at all—
in the clotted grey happenings
the sky creates
as a speculum
where foregone nature
at half mast
waits for the blue to come—
my occult promise
that accomplishes everything in sight.

Foregone's well-met
where doves regret
the life that lasts
so long in flight
it precludes what I have to say.
In a backward glance
so far so true
they forget mid-flight their target:
a mind unmasked
nature's ghost in sight.

Doves in evidence
borrow for Christ's sake
from the universe
a fatigue of fresh air.
Pressed into images

they measure absence
weigh their surroundings
as a reckoning—
I am for crying out loud
an eternity foregone.

A VERY STILL LIFE

(After Matisse)

In disguise windows are
arguments for forgetting
how, in free play, roses lilacs
bougainvilleas remember
what we might have said

in full view
of offsetting promises
shadowy futures
that in abstraction retrieve
an Eden, an enchanted
memory in free fall
our margin of error
a Utopia of sobs.

SMALL MATTER

Error in dialogue with his inner corpse
recalls words to an afternoon's regret
so that he, in a modesty of wit,
might, stammering, prolong speech
to get the better of chance.
In the debris of honest air
purloined words
like bereaved dice
fill his mirror with doubt.

A POET IN HARM'S WAY

In his dialogue with uncertainty
the detritus of fractured verbs
are lonely wagers a shy ellipsis
might celebrate
in its fond embrace
as an ornament
to the language of misgiving.
Now, as a matter of opinion,
his wily plural
confiscates
by word of mouth
his celebrity
that the annals of derision
unmitigate his silence.

TAPS FOR SPACE 2

In the cemetery of left over space
he recruits words, befriends
their history, and in despair
takes obsolescence to heart.

In a full take
each heartbeat
a word all along
that freed of his keeping
is a voice over
that takes his promise to bed.

(Under the tutelage of redundancy
accuracy is
without doubt
a slip of the tongue.)

LYING IN

Dreams honor mischief.
Lying in the lap of all reasonable hope,
they, ghetto-mouthed, spell nothing
but redundancy. A clown in the head
belies the absence of want.

In their own sweet time,
they picture mercy as a small word
whose halo, a pie in the sky
lies in the last ditch of ancestral want.

Here likeness sticks to the light
making a new shadow—
a slice of life
in quarantine
the singular lying in.

CIRCUS DAYS 2

In a modesty of face-time
he hides up his sleeve
nothing by mouth
but color-coded
his present danger.

In the same breath
he retrieves his sighs
from memory
his sad-eyed moonbeams from fate.

For companionship
he lives by himself
as an extra shadow
convalescent
in a want of self-description.

So hearts and minds
in catastrophic time
go begging.

PORTRAIT D'UNE FEMME

On stage she becomes an appetite
a flamboyant whisper
mourning what she affects.
And so astray in solemnity
adding a little silence
to the silence to be sure
her inner ear affects a moral
presumes a history, in full dress
allays in stages her hunger.

AN OVERNIGHT WITH WORDS

La pensée, c'est une image éconduite.
    —Henri Michaux

Belated in description,
his words, ornaments of a shy promise,
mourn in gratitude the inscrutable.
Truth to tell, they are if nothing
but the unforgiving
asperities of those fretful nights
that mistake heartache for meaning.
In the economy of each telltale wish
they are in their own time
like left over shadows, forgotten prayers,
that give way
along with all his artful ways to a blind horizon.

STILL LIFE WITH A HALF-TRUTH

In the debris of the unseen
his words are god-infested
hand-me-downs. Face blind,
they find in infidelity
a passing resemblance to a half-truth
that shadows withal our faith.

Here insistence is all.
In the desperate light at the tunnel's end
words become like gods
in their loneliness
their memory of the world
a makeshift image
an inconsolable echo.

IN TRUTH

Is truth then his familiar out of sorts?

Like a winded clown, he squanders chance, concludes nature by accident in truth.

A denatured world airs out his grave. Truth here dies to an inner drum roll.

In intimate default, he rummages in his mute faith. Under a cloud he claims in truth a missing part.

In the ashes of ennui, he finds in truth a wealth of being. His world a part, his faith a gallant trope.

In stealth of language, his orphan voice, blindsided by the clown in it, maps the inarticulate. Swallowing hard, he mourns truth with a piece of his mind his faith.

In delinquency, truth mirrors distance, his self a promise honored in the breach.

In the matinee of his wry endings, platitudes haunt the truth bereft of what comes next.

So he enjoins every which way the wind blows the growing of a world out of sorts in truth.

POETRY (BY ALL MEANS)

Words, bouquets of incontinence, aspire to a true vocation.

Innocence falls to the judgment of language.

Each caesura has the character of urgency. Impatient to be quiet, it disappoints.

Words that hazard the true nature of infidelity, in reflection, pursue a trope at odds.

Doubt invokes desperation as material for art.

Desolation: the deep silence of laughter.

Language matures in desperation. It mourns what it risks.

As long as absence comes to its aid, understanding persuades with art.

Art is the left over echo to be continued.

Loneliness forgets itself in language, an elegy in the making.

Doubt: a period in pursuit of what comes next.

Understanding as a lonely sequitur is company to the end

A poem is a bold proposal that keeps disappointment in mind.

In the theater of want words spoil for company.

Someone is there inside that word. Just listen.

Interpretation is a part of speech in waiting.

Poetry in the mouth of paradox impersonates reflection.

In the habit of self, words find asylum in distraction.

Truth: a fond diversion.

Laughter: an interpretation caught in the act.

Is sadness then the presentment of self passed over or a brief vacation from inattention.

A little mercy makes its way into language by all means as auto-da-fe.

—Insistence is all.
—Insistence is all and nothing.
—Davie/Cela

FEELINGS (UNTITLED)

He didn't care to know too much about what he felt. After all, as soon as you know what you feel, you feel something else.
—Leonard Michaels

A mirror quickly forgets,
gets with child, squandering how
a threadbare afterwards
escapes doubt in the making.
Here scarred dice at the foot
of a father's blue debut
practice the tail end of an oath.
(All rumors being ill-
disposed race like cloud shadows across . . .)

Is the child a fragment of a wronged
vowel the puzzle-
part of what a father forgets.
Hindsight mirrored in a virtuous
cloud begets in the eye
a performed image.
Unmatched,
it upbraids in silence
a stalled remorseful sky.

The contemptuous part of being
alone the father's wish
is a child's prurient present.
Measured by morning,
footsteps to follow—heads up –
it clouds the forecast
a mirror lost in thought.
In the wealth of his isolation
all evidence lies.

In the abashed mirror, the child's
a blur, an example made
of solitary air.
Hearsay to father one
precocious image one
drawn by lot having lost
its way finds in a whisper
a grieving echo
the biography of a wish.

It's the child's lookout
to steal from the sullen face
of reason a father's
voluminous absence.
All mirrors being incontinent,
each deplored riddance
is an artifice at risk.
It daunts likeness
but finds asylum in a wish.

Let the child stew in vicarious
warmth. Let the mirror believe
it knows more
than the reticence that makes a face
indifferent to reflection.
Such nuance is only
an alibi at first
blush the dearly parted
beleaguered by a wink.

Home forgets him like a thought.
Aflame with reason,
it ravishes
a child at heart—
father in the face—

shadowed by inattention.
Seeing things sets the mind apart,
each breath an enlarged
pause, an orphan-in-waiting.

All rhymes on duty,
aphasia counts
what a child recalls
as a wild guess.
So all his words
come true to lust
till all paternity retires.
He patrols his preface in real time
in embarrassment of meaning . . .

Is an image but a stranded look
that weathers space till a father
breaks like a lost thought for home.
A shrouded thief watches over him
measuring plenty
to forgive the face
till choked with language
all senses grin
devoured by their symmetries.

It's the mirror's gloss in the face
of getting fathers the wrong
man in the margins of a guess.
No image makes much of reason
but taking it all in
explains itself
licensed to speak
for the unrepentant
allegorical dice.

A sullen thought studies
a child-like likeness, caught
in the shadows, hand-in-hand
in a passing second
encumbered by definition.
A protest of mirrors stands by.
It evokes sex
as a wry reflection
that no one trope contain him.

Is death just back-talk
a smoking trope
where a child's likeness
downcast couples at the edge:
a burnt collage.
Here the cure for candor
suffers no curfew.
Mimesis smiles
alone on a bleak façade.

Memory scatters.
See hear how
with a wounded look
it defines depth
as deferred likeness,
and echoing the deep-end of being
a word
the child begs for,
is a minute brought to attention.

Is the child the refuge of a true story?
(No promise of narrative connects silence
with a fugitive gone stale.)
Having a home—

each mood nesting in similitude—
he regrets always
the wasted space
in his rummaging two-of-a-kind.

Fatherhood's dawning on the child's
upright postpones
in the reminiscence of a "but for"
the troubling cross-
purpose of intimacy—
its forlorn weight
the spanking farce in the face
that looks past
the law's ongoing letter.

An appearance escapes between pleas.
Overheard, it explains,
facing an orifice,
the sob a child asks after
feeling impatience out.
It overlooks a timeless
bed here a widow's
window of explanation
where all lucidity lies.

Regarding
a father addressed
all told
a summons in memory
is figured out of forgetfulness.
It ripens offstage
a benevolence dreaming
a reproach apart
empty of definition.

Father's the elegance of unused speech
the diary of the inconceivable.
A habit addressed
he strays in the mind
ready to be seen
as the heir to disbelief.
In abject space
he preens among shadows.
His sorry syllables figure the world.

A child has no idea, but seeing
as speech is married to a loss
of words, he faces once
and for all his hesitation
like an ultimatum
idling in the mirror.
Envious of empty,
he fathers a life-sized
memory honoring nothing.

Stealing parables from the in-
consolable: he maps
his embattled syllables.
And matching footprints
with signs of life,
he reasons slowly
in the face of happiness—
his manifest—
but fails feet-first in the mirror.

Are all trysts perspiring mirrors?

(Hindsight goes without
speech after all
failing a non-

sequitur in time.
It fathers an inconspicuous rhyme
where shadowing life
each word's demeanor
is the child's half remembered.)

No child in a hurry
endowed in doubt
escapes all reason . . .
But too forgetful to forget
is blind-sided by a father's
word, its terminal shadow
a silhouette
and lost in thought
is unprepared to shed light.

It is to be in name only
a sudden hush withheld
from being tongue
in cheek a bespoke corpse
that thirsting with child
is an aging mirror and eye
to eye turns a blind syllable
to the most wanted
being made to last forever.

The impossibility of describing chance
haunts his intelligibility.
But gracing the sorry difference
he, to save face,
pursues originality
as a wayward child
with no vision
fathering hope
keeps all resemblance in mind.

It's a mirror's wanton whispering
invites flesh
informs the sorry spectacle
the eye rounds out
to mingle with words and be nothing
but a manuscript of dreams—
a child's lookout—
his haunting birth's a self-
engendering eye put out to fraction.

Home is an unfinished look
for words, enslaved echoes
that take too long to die.
Hindsight grows in the breech.
Dumb with futurity,
it performs in the face
of fatherhood
a sign of elsewhere
mirrored as a horizon.

. . . is a loss to say what truth
has been like night sat up with
all thought of a child
made up to shadow life
in a stalled word
to his wise resemblance.
(What's remembered as being
a father forgets:
The economy of a long reluctance.)

A blush, flagging a ripe
surmise, eyes in a child's
wild guess a burnt offering,
a gloss on being

in a child's play
the reason that finds its way
to a clumsy shadow
beneath a whisper
a body stained with speech.

Memory to think of it
thanks childhood,
stains windows
in unfrocked space
till paternity returns
to the hard edge of intimacy
each gorgeous guess at a soul,
each inference
filling the bed with talent.

May all appearances come to light
a father to wit
a lookout to the unsaid.
(It's a lost rite
eyes a language without like.)
Memory's at it again:
Open to prayer
each syllable
backlit by inattention.

His gods are all foreplay,
mirrors with no say of their own.
Posing as fathers to unbelief,
they drive all childhood to metaphor.
A blast of silence
picturing words
in memory
nourishes a love of syllables
and times all flight to self.

Syntactically alert,
his collage in tears,
the child en route to a lost cause
husbands in reason
his afflicted shadow.
In his mastery,
he helps himself to those few words
that find in error
an economy to scale.

All true stories beckon with regret.
Their shrived words
with no belief to spare
their paternity
reflect on a mirror's
grace in being freed
of all memory,
the habit of years . . .
Let the gods pour over his lost sleep.

In charge of seeing for all to see,
words in no mood to reason
share in their long embrace
a paternity
and do not blink or else
shame a world made easy,
idol-willing, in nude space
to take a picture
and, smiling, leave it at that.

Father-watching
in pursuit of inattention
reflects a patience out to sea.
It arrests love,

corrects its look
and mindful of indirection,
protests error in a blue collage,
a memory
recalled as distance to a life-like sleep.

CHER NOMBRIL

    Because you are stupid, mild men contemplate you and grow wise. Because they cannot find you, fierce, impatient men feel you as a rumor and send you abroad to be loved. Because you seem to grow out of their strange, ambiguous dumb show, boy-men confuse you with themselves, an ascetic bride at some anonymous feast who is washed down by nightfall.

FRENCH LESSONS

    Your love is a lesson dropping its bright eyes into a lap holding hands. Your caress is a lap in which her shadow dies, the opinion of both eyes hanging their windows beyond reach. The feast a first name that joins us without looking.

    Your sex keeps looking for its own room. The horizon missed you growing up, a first name reading its message back into the space that eats away like God. You are alone and as widely read as the God, great pulse, whose penis sleeps at the window.

    Windows are the love of near-sighted Gods whose pinched looks drop like a headache from out of the blue. The horizon hangs there like a blind oath sunning itself. And the title, love, is a birthday thought that wears its navel for a friend.

    Your title is like a bed which is too short, an invitation whose ardors are bare feet leafing through. Your lips make room for the light print crossing the page. And the God beds there who loves his grip on leisure.

    The sun is a headache, a long-playing word that likes to be off by itself. Your good looks end there in a dark premise with sky in it. And opportunity drops like a first name the horizon into the mailbox.

PAGES

It's the accident that proves
The point like a window
Tearing down the hill

Or the established look of the page
That is the elbow of your room
Crossed out

Which joins reason
To that portrait of tenderness
A far cry from the scene.

Does your smile run to the back
Of your hand where delay brings up
Your gender?

And hoping to be cured
Face to face
Do we wed in the same breath?

You lie on your back
A shade of bandages, a page
Lost in thought

For life's abstract and freedom
Slips the mind
And the page upended

Reads from before
The sameness left in books.

The elbow that confides in your
Innocence is seen leaving
The page in many places

But in the corner
Like a light left on
In some illegible ghost-town

A stroke of tenderness

A profile touching
The grave of your forehead
Leaving much
To be desired.

Will tolerance be cured of us?

The page an eyelash
Planning to see
Like a new bride the pause ahead.

And to read
With no thought of sharing
Our story words
That fail to prefer us

A close call
A broadside of ghost-talk
Warning all ancestors
Lightly held

A stake in the heart
A patch of laughter
With gloves on.

Has innocence let the distance out
In care of
The sky before this one?

Drawn from life
The auspicious wed their gods,
Hide from men only
Their breathlessness

For every act is
The peer of your nakedness
That mourners return to the page
In silence.

POEM

Familiarity is in its darkroom
Like speech left with a child
"For keeps"

And if in quotes
It quietly slips away
It's touching still as in
Abstraction hand-in-glove
You let your blindside see to it

And on your feet still on your
Feet like a dress pulled up
Again and again a film
Looking down its lists of
Light sticks to you.

V
from *PROXIMITIES*

BETWEEN THE CLOCK AND THE BED

Munch/Johns

    1.
It's the method of torsos to sit at the councils of a
       dying keyhole,
And no venture comes to reason
But the more the clock reflects the more he

Quite in seclusion from his very
Thought elbows his way still one with
His glamour out of the way.

Thrilling with callers now
He sweeps through
A threshold facing
A void of dates, blinding

Synonyms beside the wish to speak.
And a thread of weather
A freestanding sob
Outnumbers his secret by showing it by far.

    2.
The clock stammers from hand to mouth.
Downwind, a bed shrinks into sight
To explore a number with redundancy.
Too close to call,
It marks the affirmation of dust.

As judicious ghosts
In parenthesis
Translate a passage from clock to bed.

3.
Do the embarrassments of feeding time
Enrich the meager ghost in the mirror?

And do we remember to remind the keyhole
That some abstentions are neighborly
While some, rising to greet
The dead-end said of dice,
Appeal to a white shadow?

So helpless to regret
These grieving armpits, wistful groins,
Helpings of deep-seated thighs,
Eyes, varying the chance
Of a shallow boast –
We are no more and no less.

4.
There are no ghosts in the sex scene
But the wry semblance of what they're out of.

With sighs, heaving
On all sides, they mark
Our wariness, keep to themselves
Each fresh rumor of belief –

An unfinished silence
A blind spot
That overcomes the past
As backdrop to bed
Without dreaming that we fall behind.

5.
Let all torsos be observant
And counterclockwise, playing for time,
Beat their retreat
To a saintliness that looks like art.

Noisy with rhyme,
Increasingly lifelike certitudes
Are the path of crosstalk
Anecdotally mortal.

6.
All fossil-thought
Seems underhanded in everything a substitute
For the feel of a life-like ghost –
A bleak re-think aghast.

And answering something to be said for
Each layer of delay,
It spreads in evidence
Like protracted sex
Inventing solitude
An embarrassed interval at sea.

7.
All clocks agree
That a hand lives on, flies
To complete its required silence
Where virtuous circles
Like clouds of gratitude
Are invitations to reach

A choice encumbered
In its bed, a phrase
Vibrating in its own blind eye

Where the sumptuous self,
Poverty-minded,
Is known impersonally as a gift.

    8.
So forthright an arrow might
Blue in the face
Find in its path a dissonance
A way out
Of a Southern snug
All it might hold
Of a stress left out in the dark.

Detachment's nearly picture-perfect.
It begs the body's red run of the type
That a far-flung shadow
Outstrip in person all narrative in sight.

    9.
Let the wall's inherent stretch
Of time, brought within art, cry out
To a flag's unerring extreme

That no heart cheat so faithfully
But a clock mistaking thought for thought –
Its reflection found in a long embrace –
Unburdens a grey ingratitude
That overlaps the wall.

    10.
The capacity of a flag is catching.
You stand to reason
An ill-phrased body
Whose angle of recreation

Repairs in summary
To a pillow of newsprint
And in the abstract
Gives up the ghost.

Out in the open, each erasure spies on a spread of theory.
Face up, it lies between
The smile of creation
Nearly missed
And a leg up
Bristling with indecision.
Your change of pace
Leaves the canvas carefully in the way.

   11.
Absent the arrow's gust
Of pleasure, the target dreams.
Sick of the sky
In the grip of its blue addiction,
It humiliates the space
A great matching life takes over
Practicing absence
As ineptitude
So wholly accurate
The air stops guessing
How the target, abandoned to abstraction, disappoints.

   12.
Does a clock prosper
Hold promise
As a hand-held target
Tainted with destination
Keeps an aftermath ajar.

About to be sacrificed to face
Accuracy as an epitaph,
All clocks slow down
To an apathy,
So open-faced, so utterly unread.

    13.
Is absence guarding the body's
Parting a mere allusion?

Taking personally the keyhole's
Quivering life-span, the eye
Circles to a bold assertion
Its punched-out target
A miracle of multiplication
Abandoned to belief
Washing its hands of all distinction
But unforgivably on time,
The old refrain
Honors the life
Too long to be dreamt away.

    14.
The bed, a misprint, ahead
Of all parting whose supplement
Is the open mouth of a clock,
An ignorance untold . . .

Broadly recumbent
The first bit of color
Thick-set like death itself
Does not waste the present.

Too helpful to be wholly tested
Proverbs are
Without further thought
Far and away
Like low-lying dice
Unseasonably merciless
Stunned but entertained.

    15.
A nude who oversleeps her welcome
Having caught the drift –
The gist of winter spilling
The weight of whiteness, hiding it
In graffiti's roll-call
Where it leaves off –
Will spread the word,
Whispering multiples to the dead of night,
The external keyhole grieving.

    16.
It's the keyhole, the eye's
Cut-out that honors candor.
All clutter downcast,
It beds in a glimpse
The obstacle to every gesture,
The pale animal who mourns the light
That lives with your candid eye at odds.

    17.
Stored in its own weight,
A collage, minding the eye's
Onesidedness,

Is cast as a stranger's irritable sign.
Tutored by confiscated lamplight,
Its ravishes mount

As an artifice
Is guided by gossip
To a memory below zero.

In a surfeit of miscellaneous handlings,
All confiscated things are cast as strangers.
Silence measures their fair share
And makes no promises but what it keeps.

    18.
No gift out of place
Explores patience
But ungrateful doubts
Have a hand in it.

Yet the theater of poverty
At the thought of words
Is lost in comparison
A hideaway to nod in.

The imprecisions of art are not evidence
But the dead-pan state of nature
Will lie at length
A fresh exception to hospitality
An invidious holder of views.

Drifting pillows, eavesdropping
Postures, eventful words
Swallowing the air –
We take strength
From objects with no bearing.

19.
Will indifference clock the threshold of description?

No shadow posing in the nick of time
While questioning at second hand
The still life heroically convened

Escapes numbering. Now temporizing
As targets must, our inattention
Recalls a zero, second hand
To the ground unthinkably foregone.

20.
Choice carried to term
By the light of a naked number
Is a monument
In the shape of helplessness,

And tired of praise for the wholly fathomed
Is confiscated
As short change
For the volume of the heart's overflow
Exactly

Opposed to language: an emphasis
That arrives too late
For the funeral of the unintended.

21.
Under the vain lamp of appearance,
The clock defers
To the temper of bedsprings
Gathering the occult vibration of a tick.

Are façades merely lethal bystanders?
Emptied of sleep, they dream
Of the sun setting
On what's been done
To the evidence
Its pride of place.

    22.
Absence in bed with
Its chronology alludes
To a number
Naked infallible
Deep in a closet of lost air.

At stake in the world,
Each allusion stranded
In the body's episodic black and blue
Holds a space open
In all humility

Comes dressed as a number,
A precipice upheld.
Incoherence
In memory rests assured.

    23.
The ubiquitous cause of a flag's enhancement
Is a just addition. Under arrest,
It pours over its lineage
Flat out prolonged in a just cause.

Hushed as a pillow
In space dreaming
A geography of fresh emotion,
This virtual bystander,

Stark where
Tradition is dressed
Down,
Is numbered in a lost cause.

    24.
Plumbed syllables of sad
Desertion, targets
Lost to the one impression
Left in the telling,
Are a feeling's blind spot
Lethal in presence.
An arrow's short shrift
Knows the small print by heart.

Yet the bow's thematic hum
Exhaling space
Prolongs disparity
Where, site-specific,
Error comes round
For *Now* face down in a sullen prayer.

    25.
Does an overflowing number need a bed-check
To embrace departure's close-up as a text?
Each concept feigning a lone figure
Is loosely flagged
To perform its sedentary phrase.
A target slumbering on its side,
It makes a clearing for all
Those minutes the so many beggars
That exhaust their artifice in passing.

26.
The target postponed in all your thoughts
Is the forerunner of what's
Accomplished in a lost cause.
One eye at a time, it keeps
The sky circling in all your thoughts.

For a long wait
Confides reading
To a memory
Whose corrosive shadow
Is the petulance of a lost cause.

Is hindsight here
But a small gesture
The distance dying in all your thoughts?
It finds its place
As a narrative
Where external grief
Is a glass darkly through.

27.
Will chance
Having wished for
A number share
Its death await
A caption in the light.

Word for word
Seeing an end to everything in sight,
Unlikeness like
An extra life
That rhyming in irrelevance
Forgets the words
Lets all the music in.

28.
The bed speeds up
A tête-a-tête
Exhales its mirror of choice.

The beauty sleep
A clock turns back
Its still tacit
Purpose crossing
Concerted bedsprings
To flag a featureless adieu.

Rising musically
Like a preening grace note
It honors the elevation of a groan.

29.
Now the clock slows down
To a wide-eyed theory of relevance
That so often taken to task
Is a spending torso
Embedded there
With each fresh look
Impartially innocent of explanation.
Alluring numbers
Like sheep count
Their ambitious daydreams
The last clock in.

30.
Awash in a wish,
Will the arrow's exit console
In practice a vacancy,

Invent space
In the tired shape of delay?
Here, in the fleet of memory,
An estranged timepiece
Lies.

There is a narrative in the air:
It counts as previous
What comes next
What, etched in the air, the mind already knows.

    31.
A pause,
Striking as an epitaph
Drawn from the comfort of a white embrace,
Prolongs a reckoning
That all loose ends abide
With a death to spare

The grief that rising to abstraction
Falls on a bed of artifice
As neglected numbers
Turn round and round
Paging themselves forever.

All apertures are gestures
Now in doubt the sum
Of all our elegies
Left out to dry.

    32.
It's the future of sunset in the sight of any crosswalk
That in his lifetime
Is an accident to name

An orange in memory . . .
Death to provide
At a moment's notice an epigram
Where the rule at random is the one
Exception to the high wire of recognition.

There are <u>no gaps in unlikeness</u>
But mixed emotions hold
In the vast pathos of correspondence
Answers to all discussions
Of the many legs of a thought the size of someone else.

PROXIMITIES

1)
    Flabbergasted so short of words,
    He measures himself as pure inference,
    A long drawn-out pronoun
    Denying chance.

2)
    Put into words, his life is
    The intelligence of a long story.
    Apprenticed to incontinence,
    His skills are mirrored to distraction.

———————

3)
    Unfaithfully present, his image,
    A once solicitous part of speech,
    Studies solitude, whipped into recognition.

———————

4)
    He detours, marries modestly
    Where a smile denies
    By no means his word's
    Artifice: a Pale at heart.

———————

5)
    His word given, a façade of freedom
    Lives lightly, a life-like shudder
    On the wronged face of a lie.

———————

6)
    Having been "he" for so long,
    A mistake so accurate
    That trusting words
    Make for a weightless marriage.

———————

7)
    Weddings that lose sight over sleep
    Are mirrors dozing till a word arrives
    To witness a wound's idolatry.

———

8)
    Having had words with
    Forgetfulness, he thought it
    Over: how marriage in truth
    Is the tearful part of longing
    Hung out to dry.

———

9)
    His flesh, being a tall order,
    Rallies to the light of its burnt umbrage . . .
    He spoiling for a happy ending.

———

10)
    His image, a wake-up to his one calling,
    Eyes in confidence what comes
    After he exhausts reason, that recluse.

———

11)
    Impressed between lives
    Words hold their own
    Their uncollected airs
    At some vague distance
    An early ear of reproach.

———

12)
    His poems pause at their own risk
    Are found wanting
    To impersonate
    A solitude for whatever else they are.

———

13)
Shadowed by guesswork,
Words come to their senses.
Backlit by coincidence,
They think aloud,
Mispronounced in his flesh.

---

14)
Eroticized as incredulity,
Ellipses hold in their lost cause
A bleak caprice, a secret
Without spilling.

---

15)
Boredom befalls a deaf ear,
Fulfills in earnest his every need
With some reason, secretly overheard.

---

16)
A watchful shadow recalls chance
As the farewell thief of old regards.
Exploring sadness,
His thoughts lie elsewhere
Ghosted by understanding.

---

17)
His career, a wasting mirror,
Calls its shy semblance to account.
A long pause in evidence,
It measures a latent ghost.

---

18)
The page, his thumb wintering there,
Turns – all life waiting –
To the telling site of reminiscence.
His loneliness an eagerness in the ear.

---

19)
His sentence, reasoning long after,
Escapes silence, outlives
Error as a dim prospect,
Wronged in the event.

───────────

20)
Is fatherhood one for the road
A pretext haunting
Its own image –
Ever at hand
A forged omission –
A self worn out.

───────────

21)
His obsession, with no hope
For a likeness, is a word
In mourning. It evokes
No mirror to share
The precocious carrion of childhood:
A sigh.

───────────

22)
Are all qualms like unvoiced orphans,
Their chronic soundings
A paradise of ruined airs,
A hospitality refused?

───────────

23)
A description attached to no word
Of his very own,
Is understudy
To a world fulfilled
With his lack of understanding.

───────────

24) Is God then an estranged window,
A hand ever beforehand
Unpresentable
An unescorted clue?

---

25) An apprentice-sigh summons
The shy pronoun in the mirror.
A rhyme in exile, it threats
Distance as an ornament
Suspended, overlooked.

---

26) His elegance
Thrown into bed is a bone-
In-waiting. All apathy . . .
No ball of fire he.

---

27) The dice go by.
Older than he thinks,
This theatre of a long pause
Finds no death
But puts all mirrors out for the night.

A CONVERSATION

For Albert Cook

A sober surplus rests in the conversation,
Enjambs at the foot of all
Abstentions all said
Rumors in blind trust
To trade oblivion for half-a-loaf
And introduce precisely
Caring a surface
Fastening in malady
On all our limbs in waiting.

Are all phrasings here
Misguided soundings
Where certitudes
Are caught within
To divide a little mercy?

VI

from *TRACES*

TRACES I

(Nature Morte)

On n'appellerait pas tableau de nature morte celui qui représenterait un cadavre; ce tableau appartiendrait au genre de l'histoire.
  – Becherelle Dictionaire National, 1862

Il faut choisir: une chose ne peut être à la fois vraie et vraissemble.
  – Georges Braque

La pensée, c'est une image éeconduite.
  – Henri Michaux

    1.
We die on our feet, as though
The constant opinion of roses just
Sitting there, drawing us into life's
Considered stillness might
(Clearing our throats) just disappear
And worldliness descend into every walk
Of life.

The privilege of flowers is to hold out
A level of persuasion, to collect
Partners whose upshot, breaking
New ground, will give pause
As a spare bed
Fathering images mistakes meaning
And life's understudy declines
To a lazy prowl.

    2.
People come to this.
They bring the difference to mind.
Pale with coincidence

(Like a blade sponsoring justice)
These flowers, the prejudice of plenty,
Draw to a close. Their straight face,
The daylong subsidy of a cloud
Shortage or a sigh holding its own.
The upkeep features a perishable side
Effect: a jar's blind faith, its surplus
Of tidiness, treating loyalty
With a smile. Here worldliness
Spreads the work.

    3.
Never mind the boredom

Comparisons bleed

As if between people

The density's catching

And the fruit curing

Still another surface creates in the open
Or whispered arrogance of a still
Life your
Side of it
Polished to an eyesore –
An incurable mask –
Like a bald spot
That keeps its place as food for
Thought the difference in plain sight.

    4.
A window, unwilling to breathe, gives rise
To the bird's effort. A pale boast
Of air or a curtain blowing
In unmotivated wind,
It gives notice
To your musing descent into
That laconic meadow where
Warmed over and over the art
Of seeming undercuts
The few conclusions that rest by the wayside
Here: they lose weight but flower
In your embrace.

    5.
The delay
Governing the consent of flowers
Questions a tyranny too faithful
To be posed.

Destiny's pretext
The vehemence of a closed book
Or a cancelled rollcall –
Pupils hurry back from their epitaph.

We lie about
It, we talk as if
The reigning peace within
The setting of a smirk would join
In dreaming like-minded game-birds, fish, fruit

Or drop with each
Passer-by the other
Shoe to get a start on life:
That distant look written down as lost
In those eyes that walk beside mine.

6.
Like wallflowers prepared
To do the talking,
All thoughts of this life
Are second thoughts.

And misgiving the right to
A rose is like the open
Desertion of a gloved hand:
Its timing off, it bloodies
Our lives and any other
Disguise occurring.

This is the place where
Household names, grateful for the view,
Are torn in our eyes between
Vast reserves of explanation
And the hospitality of two legs
Walking the aisle

In the open where
Flowers forget
The cut of a jug or fruit dish
Left for dead.

7.
My looking at it
Is a bandage saying
I am

Privately caught by a wide margin
Replacing red with
A rose on time.

We withdraw closer to one another
Replace this rose with a map
Peeled back in time.
The trail gets colder. It's our
Turn in profile to grow apart.

Seeing it through
Placing the cry that brings flowers
To heel

A guitar in the shape of
A landslide stops breathing
And deafens the wall in order
To go barefoot.

    8.
It's the first
Impression saved by the stunning
Memory of a future
That sees to it –

How clarity
Is sampled again
And again is outnumbered
In the open reluctance of a still life.

News of it
Smacks of the old-
Fashioned seamless kind
Of disguise, the open
And shut case of a look-out
Engaged in a peace too long
To be remembered . . .

As now, for example, in
A demonstration flowers
Their stalled masses leaning
All one way in the line
Of duty suffer the sweet mercy
Of a school's early closing.

    9.
Melancholy
Company keeps flowers
Fruit bordering on
Friendship as levelheaded
As schoolboys who swallow so much
They make the air shallow.

We settle old scores, as if
A slash of light could table
An excuse. Far from it!
The idea of an afterlife

Is catching. But our shortcomings,
Homesick at last, drawing
A second breath to defend
Nearness, eat out of our hands.

    10.
A window
Minding a long stay
Would like to share the rest
Of your life with the background's
Wry belief in a garden
That yawning lavishly begins to break

Away. It comes before us,
The tradition of growing – piling
Offer upon promise, the fine line

Gravity shares with the rest
Of your life – where grief raised
To be modest signs your name.

    11.
These flowers, our daily ghost,
Lower their eyes in order
To make a face. We beg to differ.
Yet our least apt shadow
Keeps after us and our shortcomings
Go on and on about life, whispering

Secrets endlessly – as a profile,
Ready to name names, will read
In your eyes the backward cause
Of innocence. Like a window turning
For another look, these flowers last
Until we're left behind.

    12.
Class is out.
But the animus in the schoolyard
Suffers no particular
Life. Its fruits
Hang on our need to know
How the other lived so long
In the forecast, how a warm embrace,
Accurate as incest, clouds the day
With a last wish to be trivial.

We survive, alas, only
In confidence, our neighbor.
As a fine day leads down to the shore
And is waved away. As a whisper,
Dropping everything, holds its breath
And lets God do the talking.

13.
Death calling for the last word
These flowers come-
As-you-are entitled
To stretch out, to excuse
Yourself, as sex is lost sight of
In the mirror. Your sole
Setback, to affront grief,
Will leave both feet awash
In other plans.

Resemblance –
Titled insomnia –
Paging the origins of daily
Life, your patience –
Where death pairs off
Mysteries of equal length
To share the preferred look
Of flowers lost to sight.

14.
As skies overlook their blueness,
The eye's
Pitfall holding
Your weight adjourns
To the grave fellowship light
Put out to pasture,

Where likeness warms to the single
Life whose fruits befall
Reds and dull greens that reach for air
To make a killing.

Is it foolhardy to stand still,
To argue bleakly that you've been
Around, that justice,
Like a spare room,
Remains to be seen?

    15.
Red is
In danger, the flowery phrase
Tactless but morally
Alert: The marriage goes on
Openly and turns on
A window's willingness
To prompt

Our bedside best
In living memory
The eyes we make
They take us for fools.

Life dressed up
As life is too
Talkative to erect thirst
As a vase defends its capital

As a rose again is told in error: Begin.

    16.
Flowers that miss getting even with everything
Like tears have less to say now and more to
Embrace as a vow or a long pause.

The table whose head
Passed away this way
Is the soul of caution.

The vase pouts
In your own words
The flowers point

And a seasoned bystander, the wall, takes it all back.

    17.
Do waves of bygones respect the sea's
Emphatic promise: a clearing?
By dead-reckoning
Between the lines
These airs are gregarious

A nest of intervals
Where delayed music blooms
And holds, red-faced, armfuls of shortage –

Old cloud-lengths
Landlocked birthdays
The pause we put in charge
Of the sea, between the lines,
Will promise us the earth.

    18.
Just when the sun recalls flat-out its perfect setting
The odds build against lunch –
An old sigh –
Where an absent-minded breakfast goes
    To break
Life's secret plan
In two.
Where a teacup
Minus a sullen teacup
Has strength to color
    You equal to
A leakage of good looks.

Half-a-loaf begs off
The distance made up
Slowly the sky dies down

Like an old newspaper that wants to spare
Your eyes.
Do you understand my silence
Now my one serving?

    19.
Is the pause that overruns the music
The same gesture neckties turn
Into knots?

    Tomorrow's
Kerchief will put up with
The violin's beheaded dash
To freedom. A ghostly head
Will stem flatly those
Notes some of these
Days die in earnest.

Now grace scores the assembled headlines
As a table without mercy
Clears all paraphrases away.

    20.
Fruits will memorize
A profusion of patience among the narrow-minded.
Their gravity spread evenly
Gathers the four walls to taste.

A heartbeat away,
The mouth-watering
Versatility of dying
Falls.

Stolen from exits,
Fruits better phrased than most
Pauses applaud
Like mirrors that dress alike.

Here hospitality is the prompt angle
Of a poem bereft
Of things.
And even if we trash the border between
The poem's leftover arrogance
And the stark impatience of fruit
Crossing our minds

Kinship remains the eye-
Opening passage
Our breathing spells.

    21.
The book no longer takes back
Unread a rose so
Pronounced between covers

It comes up deaf
As a pillow regretting
Its pastime dreams of tense

Days in the crease ahead
Where the few words dismissed
From nature are picture-

Perfect and a rose-in-waiting
As *always*
Is evidence of thought.

22.
An unaccompanied love
Of music escapes into
Nature until it looks
The same –

Proof after proof
A head
Noting the one stillness for all
Our words and their lifetime
The impatient ones
The implicit

Headlines that write the world up
To a breathless total
Stranger than fiction . . .
A fateful exception
The poem's generous mumble.

23.
Poverty is
An extravagance of language
Too wistful to live out loud.

The corpse falls evenly . . .

A meal like a shadow stretches
In order to avoid counting
Those guests of objects who wall-eyed
Pick their way among widespread
Beacons of shade, sentences
So loud as to break
Bread we have brought to earth
Within hearing.

24.
The lucid Ace at the edge
Of the table having finished
Its shadow longs to be drawn
As a target for reflection . . .

The poem slows down in the mirror
Extracts an armchair, alarms
Legs in a word sideways
And, recumbent, guides the pronounced
Ace ready to turn its initial
Doubt into sculpture.

25.
Tickets moreover trip over blindly
The bedroom
And little risks die in the
Altogether laughing behind
Our back.

Attached to this life
A short-handed judgment calls
Till a mindless red
Minds the inhabitants
Whose heartfelt trips
Might save a face
Emptied of their own choosing.

26.
Embarrassed
Flowers to quote
From all sides invite
Forgetfulness.

They are terraces of error
Like rain inscribed beside
Raindrops or spent petals written
Into a primal setting.

Losing ground, we propose
Journals thick with the room's
Inconsequence. What other news
Stays on as if for nothing?

    27.
Will she overlook the ink
That doubts her being the sole
Tense among others
Breasting

Banners of waisted words glossed over
Shadows the armed pause at the edge
Of the blanket the exchange of silence
No breath takes after

But this hide of earth
An emeritus pink
Will lie differently.

    28.
There is no narrative in sight
But events smile on

Apples unread spelling
Clockwise the feeding
Of newborn pride.

We dine on coincidence
Extend ourselves
By courtesy of their pride of place

While – thinking aloud –
They prolong freshness, mishandle
With ease the visiting rights of fiction.

    29.
In the event the nude
Enclosed in her first
Time-out –

As a sentence eyes us in one breath –
Serves, hiding in a word-
Shortage,

The ideal reader
Who empty-handed retires
Early to rehearse his first

Cliché: those blue eyes
That protect their shadows like
Commas-in-hiding.

    30.
Do words drink
Deeply in other words
Leave the impression they just might wish
To be otherwise employed?

You seem to appreciate the ceiling . . .

Whose echo-
Harvest arrests
A gap that
Flowers among eyebrows
Guessing

Which bed's extra
Patience, writing itself
Into sculpture – a white
Concern –

Is the last word
That streams, bottoms up, from your face-
To-face the enriched
Breath of emergency
Borders poured over.

  31.
Let flowers come clean
Be their own brushwork
A sigh

Or a spy prodding
Each leaf to pose as a phrase
Tucked-in or an argument
Whose sweeping intent
Settles without trace
On a heap of sunlight

Where the bed's
Upkeep – the cause behind which
All flowers unite – will make itself
Scarce in the making.

  32.
A delay
Of windows caught
Differing adds apples
To error in store for
The basket's hollow boast.

Attention gathers
Excludes life, the sad
Trespasser, adds
Candor to waiting –

To die of it
The poem's gregarious upset
A luncheon of recognition
Without remainder.

    33.
The exhibition of white
Lies in phrasing a window well shut
Of a second thought.

And wallpaper facing
The future squarely steals off
Behind our backs.

So red-handed we refresh
Apples, gathering phrases: exits
Of wounded calm, our breath.

    34.
Shadows that push nodding too far
Are loath to sidestep the light
Lunch dying down
The page. Their acquaintance holds
No more of our reservation than death
Our spare time might visibly wrong.

    35.
As angels smoothing
Feathers of sweat
Are sacrificed

In their own minds –
A chance meeting
Of long-held airs –

So apples pose
A dying harvest
And blush at being
All thumbs . . .

Maps under siege.
A sky's put-down,
Pinned syllables with a feel
For surfaces – we break ranks
And staying late unearth
The fruit from sleeping.

    36.
Music like doubt will share
To linger. Notes
Of apology like heads turning
Describe a judgment too
Early to count. A line
Of pretense, some light
Reading, will supplement between
Acts the pitch of an exit
Straining.

    37.
Still life's vestige, our inattention . . .

A pout hiding a lemon
Out at the edge of shelf-
Life limits what's kept
In the dark pocketing
Thumbprints in question

Unclassifiably thorough

No such thought stands for the eye's
Crossing a lemon back
By way of a pause, bestirred
To the end by language: a narrative,
On leave, appealing.

   38.
Is rhyme also a summer solid?

A blue pencil
Being the pick of all
Point urges stemming

Does this in memory
Of the same sorry
Angle of meditation –

The quick stab
In direct descent
Bedding as usual

Puts in the plural
The best laid plans
Lie unmolested –

Our oath's close-up
Lost in the sighting
Holding resemblance up.

    39.
It's the prospect of being spied on . . .

The carafe's
Hip, the horizon,
An immodest deadline.

Is the sum merely the place
Where the sun used to be
An occasion rising
To treat pears alone
On the page fingering
Another's privacy

With all eyes echoing after the first flush
Of freedom: being late.

    40.
Flowers idle
As tears are so inclined
As to bring out into the open
Person a handout merely
In passing grateful
That windows fielding their ignorance
Will die hard like statues
Climbing a wall.

After this
Therefore because
Of this – a perspective bent on
Making amends wears
Its colors like exhaustion
That a plague of shadows
Flowers without mercy.

41.
Will speech delivered to a large glass
Like breathing spell the correct name?

A word to forget
Its cunning thumbs through
The gait of flowers read
With beginner's luck . . .

We enroll the remote
Dice and the rest
As wintering reaches
The white plate's reward.

What's on
The table is
Ready-made
The watch word
An acquired taste
For all kinds
Of delay.

42.
Music plainly visited now
For then having long
Practiced the life of a room
Settled by old scores.

A poor historian –
Its reticence filled with
Adjacency notes all
Discernable explanations
Meeting up in the whole –
As the heart's grasp

Of an Ace edging out
Is waved off and the blue remnant of the sky's
Attention comes of age.

    43.
Interminably short
Of its true colors the news
Leaves early to stay
Put like a stream standing
For the clear-cut depths
Of a lost headline.

Felt to be near, a silhouette
Will rescue writing from flowers, fruit,
From a violin
When all that is said
Is done weighing
All headings with abandon.

    44.
Is peace the slow progress
Of lunch, an arrogance
Come alive?

The pear's ultimate
Gaze, a slice,
Broadly entitled,
A first thought
Too late to argue,

Put out to witness
The least grief:
A bare mouthful
Open to question
Its one meal eating away.

45.
Blond vegetables blunder.
The event so far
Askance as to why

A deep breath posing
In a word fulfills
A pot with a lack of memory.

A phrase jealous of something stirring
The sun's slow emphasis
Takes, in effect the first turning,

Brings to a boil
A profound look made ready.

46.
As though their deft slowness
Were skin, lemons drawn out
Enough to reflect peel off

A diligence
An inclination

Of yellows clocked to rhyme with a long reach,
Their thick haunts,
Like an illness mobilizing space,
Are the inaccessible part of leisure,
A thud beyond reach.

47.
As if death were
A platitude
An omission sharing
The soul of patience

These don't look like apples but they are

In practice being
A red threshold
The fruit's access
An aftermath –

Or a basket disarmed
By invitation itself
Swallowing first hand
Passages so
Swiftly we get them down
In memory of a white result.

We run, dying of thirst,
To the lightness of the sentence
Where the evidence, an enlarged
Fast, is a matter of days
Declining in broad daylight.

48.
Pictured between sentences, the window
As punctuation, its white understudy
Withdrawn, restores to idleness
A white embrace

Like a vase that has stopped growing
In plain forgiveness
Or childhood passing like flowers
From hand to hand –

Death's missing
Breath short of
An answer –
A blind bit of light
Its many touches
The future of unease.

    49.
How do we step out
Of character how put weight on
A time made wholly tempting
To round out this still
Living invention, man.

A matching handout –
Our daily bread
Gives us each day
An outbreak
Of windows their closing
Scene as the straight
Face a light visits like a strange belief.

    50.
Apples however distantly
Enlarge the object
Lesson of all things,
Its immaculate guesswork.

They stand to reason
Like bookends borrowing shadows
Before sleep, or clouds gathering
The visible, their stammering life-
Like habit of angels eating away.

Not to miss the point,
Who counts for us, takes food
For thought, prolongs the apple's
Incurable meagerness,
A likelihood unused.

    51.
A rose before patience only
In error the wall breaking
To that extent tables still
In name only the left
Of breakfast the least
Sign of bread accepting
A usage within reach . . .

Will a red cry look up the start
Of a sentence, the rose turn
Like a mirror listening in?

    52.

A bird signing	The pear's pulse
The air with its shy	A lap a green shade
Incumbency	Circles in flight

    A thought airing a page
    By comparison will grow
    A back to take our eyes off

    53.
A house in your own words
Figures to die
Traces, traces leading up to it –

The proffered no-
Man's land, an object
Lesson building, building

The death that missed us
From face to face
A detached tolerance lost on us

And the poem's secret following:
A piece of candor, the horizon's
Protégé within sight.

TRACES II

    54.
And idly by an apple standing
In ease of redness,
Such heedlessness in errant space
Is next to godlessness
A flat assertion –

An apple's posing in such full reserve
That questioning our solitude
Its silhouette,
That stunt of a life in errant space,
Is the autograph of a wink.

    55.
If there must be wisdom
Let it be superfluous –
A god learning to live
Without ambition.

And using people for growth
Only in that event
A thoroughfare
An apple's asking after the fact
Is a venture in not believing . . .

Vain as the day is long as
Thought's thinkable getaway
Each insight of returning gratitude
Is read to be rid of
An excess of long-awaited color.

Pick a loss, no great
Loss of outward recognition
Where a pause guessing at upright

Puts a heart in its place
And lingers now
There is no pleasure in not being tired of it.

   56.
A mirror
Troubling to know
Its silver lining.

Art grows impatient
Its unemployable pulse
A lost reason for life.

It backs off
As the all-knowing second hails
Each weathering glance
A simile.

Now apples that let
Their irritation show
A sphere of influence

Like pallor, that last farewell,
Are on their own
Here where indifference stands
For the last gasp offered by heart.

   57.
A slice performs briefly
Verticals of a deep
Blue irritation of apples
Where extracting color
From the word-abandoning whip of syntax
Is an illustration of the poem's own time.

Its honored silence!
And staring down
An extravagance of space
It preserves reason
Stripped to a blue result.
So apples are
An abuse of longing
In anticipation, a late arrival,
A blue streak
Gradually on time.

    58.
No word into fruit shrinks
But makes a mountain
Out of shape from holding
Our one step at the rate
Of a sweet sorrow. The table's reckoning
Keeps at pleasure its metonyms
Under a cloud, and eyes between
Envy and boredom a home
To doubt its proof of stamina:
Its voluptuous dismay.

    59.
Snug as a peach in a thud,
One thought fits all
Eavesdropping on all the shape we can absorb.

With a generosity given to
Reflect the future,
We treat a peach punctually with understanding.

Behind the scene,
Recognition is in the air!
A sinking feeling
Harvesting scruples
An elegy to suspicion.

60.
Do flowers at bedside not to be believed
Embrace the language of substitution?
Far from thought, we consult
Color to give grief
A pause of unlikeness
Askance showing the way.

While sleeping on it, fate
Smiles on the face of it
A punctual shadow
The last familiar
Lost in nuptial space.

61.
At table not to be dismissed, allusions
To a red-faced lifetime are homesick,
Generous with inhibition.

Credulity,
Breathless in your face,
Makes up a future

Wanting to drop in
Where apples are
So firmly held that no suffering – no voracious
Platitude – devout at table
Drops out of sight.

62.
Breakfast goes without grace
Is prone to paraphrase
A solidarity beyond
A besetting distance.

Thoughtlessly on time,
It arrives
(Having lost its footing
In the fine dust of submission)
Like an aphorism
That piously overcast
Returns to its fasting surfaces imagining sleep.

   63.
Apres le bain

Does the company of discretion
Stem from a shared thought
The draft of a white embrace?

The nude ahead of
A great sadness
Has no standing before life
But idling in description there
Submits a thigh in hiding
Each look in advance
Of a great sadness
That no sex settles
To overlap
Water closer than tears.

   64.
Do increments of sex
Take place on a plate –
Pastiche like a bed under observation?

There's no telling
But having to hand it
To exhausted pears –

A great stretch all black and blue –
It's the clarity keeps us dying
Where all crosswords

Denounce description
And a wet skull recites each
Syllable excavating laughter.

    65.
The line, a broken hangdog smile,
Cuts to a bleeding heart.
Read aloud, it appeals

To the same lack of muscle easing
To weigh beyond
The incest of recognition.

Here a growing conviction
Defends in the first person
The same red with a purpose

And the mark
Stunned by a white wall –
The deficit farewell –
Takes heart.

    66.
It's the language of luck that oversleeps
Each interval. Older than it seems,
It exceeds in apathy its generation.

Living with apples, it peels off
On the trail of an ornament
And falls gossiping to the ground.

Drawing parallels
The time apples are found wanting
To spell out
A faithful rendering as distraction
To serve an appetite,
All chance of enhancement by the way.

    67.
Collage has no eyelids.
Its look embraced in a rush of exits
Is the sum of impertinence
Where each word offered to a loss of honor
Has more faith in the moving
Ellipsis of this sadness
Than a hinge in doubt
Will grasp a detour in such evidence
As proves impatience before delight.

    68.
Space pronounced partial
To green is stored
As a cloud in a pear . . .

It figures duration as patience
Mirrors in guarded colors
The limit of the world
A syllable
A sidereal leak
The pear cut short
Soon to be measured for a cameo appearance.

    69.
Airing it all
As curtains dare an overdraft of pears,
Each article of light
Adding a word to please space
Turns up as another spelling.

Taking its weight for clarity,
Each afterthought –
The heft of a hand-held childhood –
Has the last word
That goes to where a door is missed in tears.

Desire's orphanage!
Here a word lives on from hand to mouth
Like a self-inflicted ghost,
Open to the prevalence of pears.

Is life, having hired out
Our eyes, a truce made
Of refuted similes?
Still in the mouth's diaspora
Our chronic domesticity,
A green encumbrance,
Is ready to be born.

    70.
Domesticity lingers, consoles
Chance exhausted
In a bowl of auspices . . .

While pears dreaming their prosperity
Hold in advance an Ace
At heart: each shadow refuted,
Calls all colors in.

Will proximity
Break into words
Each poor illustration
Then temporize
What pears choose to remember?

71.
This hesitation, the sex of solace . . .
These flowers head for the next expression
Of waiting. Our asides
Steal from their shadow
An opinion of treachery
While the slow drama of adherence
Holding its own within culture,
Is a hand-held welcome.

Does each flower
To give something away
Know the fascination
Of a lasting hygiene
A relief
To commit murder
To memory, to make use
Of the world, its cutting
Edge – this dying
Arrangement adds to our former selves.

72.
Let words apply the dead of daylight
To the snug of a peach, the bulge and its confidant
In desperate contrast
To the expiration of a hand.

This filibustering errand,
A prevailing weight of apprehension,
Like the gloss of an epigram
Is utterly misgiving.

So being precise –
Each exertion in place
Of a skill – visibility,

Its sleeplessness intact
In language, like avarice
A reminder.

    73.
Now apples, now pears
(An inescapable frame of mind)
These predicates,
Now lingering, now wandering in color
Remain the picture's dire aporia.
For all we know,

They flow from the green's impatient splash
Then own up to
Impatient borders
Where studious as a beggar's choice of shadow
All escape insouciance
To forget themselves
For all we know
A damp recognition
Subtracted from their names
An elegy to suspicion.

    74.
Such is the force of habit
That quiet makes bold
The devolution of a nude
Athwart a shy notation
To a phrase
That sight unseen
Is stuck with itself
Chafing against pity
Adrift in sequestered sleep.

Here the incapacity of the sentence
Is laid down
Next to the summons of time's intern
Where bedclothes unblinking in their vague vintage
Prolong their one festival: her calling.

    75.
Cast into lots
With the heart going out
To the history of whether apples
Compare – eyes to the wall –
Their solitude
To signs of unwillingness
Caught in the plural of assent . . .
Here's the crying shame of an echo trying
Each moment and looking back to judge
In the kindest light what it looks like –
A belief without sequel.

    76.
To erase is to raise beyond compare
The red repetition of an apple's
Store with no head for rectitude.

Such singleness on the face of it
Mortally numbered
Is the privilege of syntax
Where all objections to what's been read
Are privately foreign.

    77.
Foretaste of apples circling
Whatever color is obsessed
With the rule of shadows
Thumbing through bedclothes

The aura of fledgling fannies
Beckoning – all smiles –
Where the kitchen bottoms out . . .

A presumption of appetite
That all memory is self-serving,
That shadowing syllables
In an unpronounceable whisper,
Is a last write
In inconsolable time.

   78.
Each apple a day
Ill-disposed over time
To serve a smattering
Of (unfinished) ignorance
Is home grown
A long memory
Counting the time
It paints itself
In endless farewell
Each hapless essay
A corner of forgotten intervals.

   79.
With breath to spare
These apples are
Like dice flaunting
All thought at a loss
Their falsity
Now better viewed
As the first impression
Of a pronoun dreaming
Of unsaturated space
In the dark attic
Where no color applies.

80.
An abuse of cheese abides in a long pause
All parallel tastes . . .

So an apple's grimace
Appears red-faced,
A naked figure
Copying our demands,
A palimpsest of candor,
Using everything in sight,
We describe space –
All rhymes under arrest –
As the punctuation of our progress in a word
Where all engagements meet
Their previous estrangement
And head for
The last expression an apple wears out in hiding.

81.
The pause seen borrowing a missing plate
From the stunned lap of a pear
Is now in keeping

With our living daylights – ahead
Of that lassitude where mere lunch
Is lost in the midday rue.

Here life when you look at it again,
Once in variation, once in hand
Holds a candle to no lesser life
That left undercover like an article of faith
Sleeps furiously on the road to perfection.

       82.
The eye troubling
To abbreviate
At the apple's core
A thoughtlessness
Is left waiting
In its discipline
For an idiom at large

Whose vulnerability
In the telling of a glance
Is red at length
Sedated in the everyday
To withhold an exit.

So eyes wise to the brevity of thought
Go incognito in a stain of air
To steal from the outskirts of poverty
Their fair share
Of boredom in being
What apples slow down to in happiness.

       83.
Pears because of their prosperity
Picture more stealth than is needed
To mourn the hard look
Of an assignation.

Gathering all thumbs
Their dice-offerings.
We stay on, doubting
Their inexhaustible sleep.

As pears in correspondence are
Like words objects of imitation,
Each day stretched out
With a fresh pear
Speaking of love
Is an interval remembered.

    84.
Visibility confined to the last word
Falls out among pears
And tongue-tied in voluminous halt
Blinks

At each fond fragment tucked there
By its own lights
In a state too long for this world

Is a veiled attempt at stillness:
A full tilt
Having lost its head to a safe resemblance
In the middle of a thought that by other means lives on.

    85.
Credulity strains like a pear
That slow to nourish
In all likelihood
The death of stagecraft
Is the festering abstract probity
Where green reflects
A shy equivalence
An undying procrastination.

On the prowl, words
In order to put likeness aside
Are a bright forgetfulness

Whose provocation
Confident in all emptiness
Is on the spot
A head-turning meditation.

    86.
No rose arrested
Abandons sleep
But each trace of a thorn
Will keep its word
Siding with a red outburst

That marks matter with irrelevance
In the present tense
A short cut
To the mercy of translation.

Will ineptitude entice the world
To study in the hot sun
The plural? The rose, awake
To its fatality –
Its indigence now tired of all narration –
Outlines a ghost's studious
Choice outstretched.

NAVELWATCH

For Jean Arp

Coiffeur of innocence!
This homesick cloud looks up
To you, plucks at a white
Ceiling.

Your hairline
Grazing openly as an equal
Loves to consult the wall's
Cold start and climb
Every beard of air.

These print-outs harbor
To a standstill the life-
Like pieties of lost
Breath the first
Person whose uniform
Fate is a shortcut
To forgetting.

THE TOMB OF MALLARMÉ

A farewell within
The letter of the pause
Dice the result throws out

Regards only
So long-
Lived

Quotations lost in their readiness
Voice comfort for years

Now words thicken
A truce among futures
Your career merely

The interruption
The horizon, that overcast eavesdropper,
Has shaped to shelter.

THE PAUSES

When the weather's complete
And the bird unlearns its calling
A branch like a long pause will come to stare

At memory's flight
Left out in the cold
Dissembling a sky just to be with us –

A still extant
Confession without words
To spare birdsong, alas,
An explanation
Without repeatable witness.

*

The branch preoccupies
A choice used over and over
Again as a bird compels
A heaven's bright blue vocation
Arising in a wink.
It's a thought following
Carries the pause upright
Till a branch drawn to fly distraction over
The error of birds
For eyes only
Seems years.
Then a pause a photograph
Let's say a gathering
Of years around
Something to look up
Our own promise
A gift over time

(A bird's only thought
To live to see)
The punctuation of someone
Missing.

*

A bird keeps pace with
A brevity that outlasts
Once more in hiding
Everyone's mind, a clue.

Is forgetfulness here
A lookalike
The order of the words –
Their weariness aside –
An illustration
That smoothes the way
From word to word
To a fresh defect –
An unyielding narrative
Named out of existence.
A pause circling
Its unperformable shape
Accepts no word
Of its own reach.
The bird's a protest
Too visual
To seize the sky's
Percussive shore
Come loose
There to measure limb
By limb the branch
Marking a stark resemblance.

*

The bird's breast is our own
Sweet sway, its best offer
For all heads lost
Inaudibly feeds ellipsis.

Forbearance sits for that pause.
But all words are wasted
Where rumored clarity is bird-
Watching itself a perfect shadow.
Undercover of speech,
The pause, a vestige
Of two minds, will
Punctuate an assertion of pure
Need and owe to each name
The error of fluency
Its dark impostor:
A posthumous singular
Inventing nothing.

*

The bird's upshot
Lingers, shakes loose
An exit to bring attention
Back and so forth
Personify a witness.
Each pause in hiding in profile
Heads for a fresh manifest
Itself a pronoun's shortage,
Its origin in description –
Eyes making out –
What's thought.

VII

from *TAPS FOR SPACE*

TAPS FOR SPACE

Wenn unser Horizont nur der Horizont unserer
Kritzeleien ist und auch bleiben wird?
                    – Gunter Grass

    I.
It's up to
A lot of birds
Still quote
A few words like China in a low voice
I script I eat
Of old girls up
And down a scroll
Memorizing *Lunch*
Comes up again.
After the newscast, we left
To undress, enlarging
The annals of the Pekinese
Our uncombed shadow
Ready to go
On the menu . . . Here the light
Just free of its vows
Strokes the landscape like a beard.
With all apologies to distance,
We take the Chinese out-of-doors to bed.

    II.
We've learned in the headlines to achieve space
The sky, the earth, the air
The line the applause hangs on
The honeymoon and all
The room we need to leave
Our headlines on the pillow.

III.
A flag goes up (and the whole exposé goes sailing
Up the flagpole)
The clouds gather in the same sense
Explaining the day
By not being absent.
We think of the news as much as we can
And diet on the same address.

Hanging about colloquially
As a meal rises
To meet a familiar face
We catch the landscape going steady
Like rain,
And decorate the Chinese
Space, slip into the room
Like a lesson

Which looks like sunset if
We read on, enrolling
The sky, how it looks
To the flag, how a honeymoon
Lives off the countryside.

IV.
A few winks more surround the audacious gap in the lesson
For the same reason we follow the flag into space
We guard the silence like a word
That drums at the top of the page

Under the axe holding hands
For poise only, expecting to miss you again . . .
The date like a ticket that won't go far
Leaks into a blue
Encore . . .

A yawn rolls over the top of the drum
Keeping your eye as I
Am always peeled and
Ready to have you
Over
The top of the page.

"THE MAN"

For M.L.K.

From some distance
Now
The news of
You in authority
Now reflecting your dream
Will be rolled up in-
Side beside us

Now
The answer is not
There are metaphors
Seen as if through
Helping hands
Holding us up
To the light now

The humdrum is open
To question our freedom
Now demanding
Surfaces are near
Demands when
The eyes are in
Attendance

Figures do not
Lie
Down postponing
The image of hips
"Hanging on"
Like the average head
In disbelief.

IMAGES OF VIETNAM

   1
         The snapshot
Announcing China will pay
For the light including
To wish to live in

The theatre is not
For everyone gathers
In memory . . .

Halting returns to the right
Word watching
Over us night and day

   2
Opportunity overruns us
So we stay signing up
In the sky we guide
Upstairs
Taking our place

Beyond the distance knows
Our flying's of no use . . .
But what of the hands
Recruiting the whites of our disappointment

   3
No, it's not fair
The news
Looking up from its uniform
Heading for

There is the present
Handing the inhabitants
Having hands

A gun practicing
Something we felt out
There beyond the wave's
White bellyful.

STAYING HOME

All of the maps have gone ashore
Windows looking out for themselves
They are posters now they are
Wallpaper stretched out among friends

No wonder footsteps go back to
Thinking
Accidents have nowhere to go
But home

We relax with the late news
The walls change feet
The ovation stands
For the facts are there to join us
For the difference the future
Will find us hanging
Offhand figures of speech

The answer to travel is to
Raise children like windows
That, accepting their transparency,
Rise to the illustrated innocence
Of bright eyes as a chance
Of rain

ON THE FRONTIER

    I
China has come out of the rain
Whose nodding fatherhood of words
    Made light of it
Extending the autobiography of
    Knees made fluid

It's clearing up
Now that memory has left
Its shape
To the pillow-flow of numbers
Snowing light

    II
Perhaps nothing more will cross their minds
The distance their possession
Keeping house
Among the senses

But the weather is flowing among the numbers
Whose ancestors rained
Daily
Those signs of clearing
Offered themselves
    At night
    Wrapped in
Clear eyes like blind flags

    III
They advance on
Their portrait heads
For whatever reason

Its airs are ready
To leave their senses
Like rain falling
For naught

Everyone is looking into the weather
Facing the one who is
Swimming far off
He belongs to
The distance the added light the wall
Going out we added.

OLD HAT

In the heat, old hat
Our debts are running after it
The calendar keeps raising dust

Around the corner

And freedom is held up
The small print describing
A date to follow us home

For freedom is nothing
But the whole day
Like marriage itself
Watching the sunset wanting the dark
To decide

Is fatherhood climbing up
The wall the small talk
Not caring to see
The race was meant to be worth it?

We are starting to stroke
The dead heat
Fatherhood like freedom running out.

READING OURSELVES TO SLEEP

Do we learn to read from our excuses
Deliberately halting with each caress?

The procession now the lesson
We're use to
Words turning up
As empty planes
Mistake the airport
For the promise of a lifetime

Reading in bed
We watch words like
Freedom crossing the page

And over the hill
Stretching it
Till the sentence says where the tears come from
Fiction without end
A sad joke or a worse warning
A window with nothing to do

Planes eat plane-fare
Dickens Trollope the rest
Cure thickens as the plot
Looks up
Names without a clue

To yourself
Really the uniform
Light that soloist
Saying "Good Night".

STILL LIFE

For Paul Celan

A cut-out
A convalescent sky
On its way to you

An eye for the il-
Literate mouthful, the shadow-
Retreat candle-deep
At your end

Clouds draw themselves
After themselves
And in the suicide of the used
Light your wood sleeps off
Its final shadow . . .

But after a few steps
A parade of detachment
Coming out
To begin to pace
The storm behind your eye
That like the day's wash accepting
The horizon
Is the impression of your flesh
Flagging.

SELF-PORTRAITS

The painter looks out at us from behind his painting and warns us not to use so many words.
  – Paul Klee

HOPPER

The beginning of the world
Looks back

And all similarity all
That gets in the way
Like an axe that escorts
Fair weather and brushes
Your whereabouts

To get it right
Between the eyes . . .

The cool sob of a young
Porch – its absolute pitch –
Sides with an early doorpost.
And the age of the keyhole

Feeding the light feeds
As go-between
The unassailable white
Flag that surrenders your place
And lives as you never lived.

CHAGALL

This illustrious hum-
Bug that gives its head to
The villagers who ask for
And ritually get theirs
This dying fall this
Side of music: sheep   chickens
Cows   inherent in your every
Handhold creep
Into the bridal suite . . .

Their breath tunes up
Your knockdown insolence
And sweeps you off your feet
Leaving all distances behind.

SEGAL

   I.
The day's lookout is an anecdote

A walk-on
Deprived of ignorance
And no blush stays at the source . . .

Is death something between
People, a near-
relation weighing in?

   II.
If we overstay
The crossing we walk
A witness whose standing is
On the way back.
For it's only natural
To WALK DON'T
WALK past
The sadness of illiterates who light up
The traffic while dozing off
In the amplitude between.

DE CHIRICO

The sky that concludes
Openly these cool lines
Of unemployed
Regret

Will treat each scalp
Of evening
Like a stitch in time

As a dream of justice descends in a stage whisper
Its slant found in the courtesy of repetition

Is a shadow that airs its about-face
Or a platitude, its blindness cleaned,
That puts its breath back
Before it breathes on us.

HESSE

As if it had taken you
Grass-high at your word
The wall stripped to the waist breathless . . .

Will the rope on your breath
Repair space
The loose ends taking the air
As a hobby
Keep the forecast from affecting life?

(We say it's curtains
For the low profile
Inscribed like a window in unwedded
Light.)
You choose yourself as a sail
Goes sailing,
As a rope, a little spell-
Bound in innocence – the wall
Beside itself – drops
To the ground, exposes

The way you once undid your dress
So that a life might stretch out
And a slow leak come back
Smiling.

MIRÓ

The horizon on all fours
Too modest to be anonymous
Asks for the moon

And copies it.
Glued to the air from inside
A burning closet

Where halos of the same mind
Tease
A hair pursued by all planets
Painting into a corner
The chaste overtime that keeps track.

NEWMAN

Clarity
Drawn like a second wind from behind
The eye's backache
Hangs in the air
Like a prayer
Feathering your appetite
A white way-
Station. You strip
From the dove's oversight
Its aversion to all horizons.

How bored white is
As it waits, hangs
In the fire, breaks
Into crowds, forsakes
An end to loneliness.

ROTHKO

The wall's deaf side-
Show prolongs the sky's percussive back-
Talk

An asylum
Of running colors
A likeness in no hurry

The outskirts a bleached heirloom

And distance like everything
Else in your eyes, its pulse
The complicity of lightening –
Having been ruled out –
Leaves the room without speaking
An exit
That illustrates your breath
To bits.

AVERY

These smoke-edged
Foothills you own up
To are the light-hearted
Dunes that hold
The evident blue about
The buttocks harmless.

The weather you sit next to
Has views too.
It skirts the compound pinks that rock the sea

Like laughter sorting the laughter out . . .

And schooled to milk each shadow
One by one
White flecks filter through the morning talk.

Such happiness
Plainly a cow loyal to the left-handed
Seagrass edging out.

TWOMBLY

It's the magic of unreason
The look of language warms to a narrative of spilt milk
Its lingering lines
An horizon hesitant to share.

And wide of the mark
The empty name
Is an intimate of chance

Where no ink cares
To say your tears
But a loss of words,
The apparent reason, grammar,
Is what we stare at.

MATISSE

      I.

Your space
Building its bluff on the sky's
Front line
Backs into the breeze
Blocking the elbow's stand-by
Blue to invite comparison

Like a deep thought

Implanting luxury in the wild
Beast whose airs
Caress in escaped gardens those flowers
Named in bed.

      II.

The occupation of scissors
Sheds light, and the hole manifest
Beside itself, a small wonder
In the wake of an appetite,
Falls into the hands of unease –

A living god
Whose fatigue is paraphrase . . .
Like a butterfly at the edge of a disposition
The sinking feeling
Follows you out of church.

GOTTLIEB

The child enrolled in your spare time
Maps the darkness with a straight face,
His storied speech
Comes back as color for another look.

An out-burst out of adult
Hearing –
Your illegible days
Like back-talk
Go to the wall
Like kindling.

ARP

Coiffeur of innocence!
Homesick clouds look up
To you, pluck at a white ceiling.

White goes with
White looks after
The incontinence of kinship
More trusting and therefore more
Forgetful.

Your stepping-stones
Hosting the outline
Brief us like sex
Reckoning slowly but incorrectly
Birthdays foaming out of little cloud-pots
Huddled in short-lived candor.

MAGRITTE

Accident-prone
Like a shadow lending itself
To watchfulness

You let yourself down
Gracefully, an embarrassed
Presence, rising
Only to the bait of night.

A baffling memory of shoes
Smiles at our impatience,
At how close we are
To the window facing the light
Waiting for the lights to go on.

CÉZANNE

     I.

Duress
Of landscape's beheading
Close-up is definition of
Sky as near-
Miss

And immobility as rumor of pure sidestep –
Your roads lose sleep at the sight of land.

Its headings
Abstract hills rooftops rocks trees
Tossed up like a sidedish or a massacre . . .
Farewells burst forth at the first coupling.
The sky falls out among friends.

     II.

If there are dimensions to be given
Away then charity begins with
Nothing that meets the eye
Nothing more widely embrace
Than pacing the floor
Or taking sides like the shrug
Of a dead weight with the incoming
Hillside as it turns
Out, its dark footage
The feature of light that nearly runs
To fat

Or a foothold dreaming within
Your reach, taken in like a friend
On the grounds of not knowing
How the blue upright supports like night,

The unfamiliar...
You lay a hand fatly
Your gift within sight
Of the earth's unprincipled core.

RAUSCHENBERG

Will the laundry calling for your conviction
Escape the evidence with nothing on?

(The exact jubilation of a shadow of a
Habit is a holiday ready to be lied to.)

The sky beds down in a few words
The look-out answering absent
Is the pulse of your late wardrobe

And the thin confiding line you imagine
Breaks
Flush with the hammer of your wound . . .

The bed-rock
Is a guest-calling
For a final facing
As the blue dice of your iris empties with a single beat.

KLINE

An abridged
Letter comes to itself
Torn like a crown
From each erasable errand.

And black-
Listing the wall
You impersonate
You frown at how white it is

For a thought
Her silently dying to get away.

BALTHUS

The light that matters
Teaches calves how to link
Their grief to a green thumb.

Like an unused hide-out
A cat
Puzzles your nakedness
Tears at the throat
Of a child. Unconfessed,
She refuses your name
Confessing.
This orphanage of bruised air
Is shadowless –
You have no part in it.

SCHIELE

A chair at sea
Clings to your hips, bones, line-bound waste
To join again the absent
Bedstead to enrich the back
Of your hand –

A precipice
Mounting a black insult
Discharging an arm, a leg.

Accused haunches flare like nostrils
An index to
A beached hardship –

Nudity is your impatience
Singled out.

GIACOMETTI

One-
Sided the sky is
A standing coincidence that's man
Enough to stride over
His whereabouts.
It comes up short
His past
Narrowly placed
Like light shrinking in the light
Of a tall tale

Erasing
Nothing that draws the spirit up
Nothing that comes to an end.

MALEVITCH

Headings that square
With each address are tucked
Like a bandage in stored space.

(Here's an invitation to tip one's hat to
The edge of a tactfully put inclination.)

Your God, fluent but unquotable,
Plucked from the air like a stage whisper
Expands to a narrative of surveillance
Out of sight.

BRAQUE

Will peace keeping guide
Face to face
Your cutting edge?

With your doves
Musing over names for swiftness
Speech is no nearer than coincidence.

The ground parts from hearsay
As a bride backing off
The wall flattens hope absorbed into being
The depth of your conviction
The inaccessible act of repetition.

OLDENBURG

An embarrassed clarity thickens the shade
Of an overweight schoolyard. Destiny
Calling for softer nouns,
Drapes itself over distinctions
That go into hiding –

Lessons that pour over
And over your outrageous silence
Like spilt milk
A toast to your health.

AN *APRÈS LE BAIN* LITHOGRAPH

The ink of your nakedness like a starved ghost runs to your side

The horizon facing
Your face
Flickers in stone pleats

Its pallor the uprising
You meet
The sigh-proportioned list of light
The punctuation that stammers.

As you dry at a stone's throw
Your childish silence, the light crust
Afraid to grow old
Turns to you . . .
And running from side to side
The frivolity of water will read
Your mind like a raised hope
In the lap of the horizon

A vernacular blue blow that makes you visible.

FRESH WIDOW

        (Duchamp)

Private airs
Of kinship squaring with your endurance
Become an eyeful

As green
Pains the widowed
Surfaces that freshly set
Apart
Shades of outrage
Glued to an open-faced recipe
For dying away.

You lie back
Sight-reading among seams
Of obligation . . .

All alterations, unshaken in their lusts,
Mate with the Queen of Night.

ÓTAGES

        (Fautrier)

What matters feeds
Beyond the apple of your eye
An extra mouth, a ditch
Measuring the earth's
Holdings –

A living end –
A brown bag stuffed with one meal
A few feet from the fire.

CÉZANNE'S APPLES

For company
Handling each blush
With a shy man's sudden
Certainty –

A basket
Repeats within reason
A stretch after tears,
Your patience
Arguing apples.

ODALISQUE

      (Ingres)

A bather overslept
Her shadow – angling for another
Round . . .

The outline you took out
To finish breathing
Fell in

The glare of a keyhole
Gathering no
Shadow but a grey
Lash
Proof-reads your one heartbeat
Idling behind . . .

And circling beats you
To the soiled bed
Like sweat turning over
Its shield
To the skeleton of the reason that clouds you over

THE CONCERT

        (Vermeer)

For money upstream
This string of light undoes
The lightly wed –

A blind guest-
Like fidelity, a map-
Shaped handful

In the shallow of their chalk-
Dream drawing apart
A window pauses for the water's lesson

Eye to eye: a hush
That keeps its promises
And sweeps its hallways with mirrors

LE DÉJEUNER SUR L'HERBE

The horizon the lunch puts on
Is likely to peep out as
The history of this or that
      Shadow in which
        We choose to undress
We throb in the distance like a toothache

Their performance will skip
The subject will have to
Have earned its
Living like a holiday
We want to exist

It's the possibility of reproducing
The anniversary of the eye's
Being there "you're mine"
The handshake managing to fall
Behind
The landscape holding the world's
Record repeating itself
After lunch.

THE CHINESE TRADE

La tua irrequietudine mi fa pensare . . .

Those mornings we disputed
The damp aviatrix and her understanding of menus,
We dieted without example
On the painstaking applause of insects
Exchanging refrains
In the unrivaled atmosphere of Peking.
Yes, you were inventing
That amorous headhunter who hurled himself at the pilot
While ordering breakfast . . .
Our shadows unfurled there hopelessly
Like two flags contesting
The most mentioned and roomy headpiece
For sale . . .
And you, a fable, told to the other salesmen,
Impossibly continued.

ALLOTMENTS

Sparrows ad lib could stop up a chimney,
Mating I guess mid moments that might be blessed;
Vogues among ardors and oaths according
A drowse of bird-stuff slammed in the matinee.

Catch catch catch we are darlings all
Mi-fa's adrift "the matter dropped" a sigh.
Heads on our shoulders after many adieux
The host's lucky career zeros in an eye.

– *The trouble with you dear is you talk too much!*
Hopeless "a man in my position" dreaming.
– *While I, while I the strong and silent type . . .*
– *Go stand on your head dear but keep in touch.*

Withdrawn like a mother's flight to the extreme,
Sparrows in unison like a blind alley . . .
– *Nothing personal dear it's only a dream*
And a passage for all the birds missed badly.

A RACE OF METAPHOR

Periodically placing the awkward child
After the fact is family for no
Separate inflection but another child's
Willing observance of the wise perhaps,

Who must have been the last ones wholly served
Of children several deep in the thinking,
Or else who supports the issue in fact
The body bares in its quarter with plenty?

By mixing instinct with power that is
Unseasonably wrought with self-regard,
The burden of body in fact divines
What none could observe in a child like this.

Bounty by reason and the squatter's right
Comb our still surface flat. Misfortune is
Devoted indeed to the child set against
The revolting illusion of what one ever needs.

And the ruddy scholar who affronted us
Smiles from his dream and no advantage mastered,
Depriving the child as he avails himself
Of nobody else in fact his trying nature.

A VERSION OF PASTORAL

Tale's expressly fluent where Bo-Peep would
Relax. Sheep are a headache who increase
A wealth of green (who else are understood
To have the leisure to propose a peace).

Soberly outside virtuosi sing . . .
In progress Crazy like a politician
A boy's detachment is an awful thing
Happily trails off in the world's opinion.

Sicilian summary's apparent. Tails
And other loose habits of nature being
Their motion's matchless trait. A boy entails
Pronounced grass roots and topics perhaps freeing

Minds (remarkably) from backward matters.
In the deep of thoughtful green beneath the green,
The viewers asking aid of interviewers,
Sheep agitating contact are routine.

Crazy resorts like Bo-Peep to the fields
(Scholars both rampant and crashing in daylight)
Through the medium of shepherds a plot yields
Those active behind them who broadcast right

Out of this world the average sheep's delight.

CIRCUS DAYS

Are we taught
To lie
In the lap of all reasonable hope?

The humor keeps coming across

The horizon the clown
Let go
Is only justice
Passing through hands
A sigh holding its breath

A slice of life
A great smile coming home
And the likeness sticks to the light
Making a new shadow

As we help ourselves
On the way to the trip
Darkening our doorstep
Just dropped off
An open mouth
An horizon to see us through.

ABOUT THE AUTHOR

Aaron Rosen was born in Utica, NY, and was educated in schools in New York and California. He has published five previous collections with The Sheep Meadow Press, *Taps for Space, Traces, Proximities, Reluctant Mirrors: New & Selected Poems,* and *Prowling Sequiturs,* as well as a chapbook, *God Song: A Grieving Simile.* Formerly on the English faculty of the State University of New York at Buffalo, where he also served as provost, he now lives in Boston and Sarasota.